GREAT
BRITISH
SWEETS

Also by Adele Nozedar

The Hedgerow Handbook

A History of Old-fashioned Confections
and How to Make Them at Home

GREAT BRITISH SWEETS

ADELE NOZEDAR

◨ SQUARE PEG

Published by Square Peg 2014
2 4 6 8 10 9 7 5 3 1

First published in Great Britain in 2014 by
Square Peg
Random House,
20 Vauxhall Bridge Road,
London SW1V 2SA
www.vintage-books.co.uk

Addresses for companies within The Random
House Group Limited can be found at:
www.randomhouse.co.uk/offices.htm

The Random House Group Limited
Reg. No. 954009

A CIP catalogue record for this book
is available from the British Library

ISBN 9780224095747

The Random House Group Limited
supports the Forest Stewardship
Council® (FSC®), the leading international
forest-certification organisation. Our books
carrying the FSC label are printed on
FSC®-certified paper. FSC is the only
forest-certification scheme supported by
the leading environmental organisations,
including Greenpeace. Our paper
procurement policy can be found at
www.randomhouse.co.uk/environment

Printed and bound in China by C&C Offset Printing Co.

This book is for all of you who are ingenious, enterprising, and eccentric, whether you like sweets or not.

Included in this number are the inestimable Liam, Saoirse and Colm, who all like sweets very much indeed.

Also embracing these qualities are Eve, Milo, Miranda, Mia, Saskia and Willa. Ditto.

And my good friend and travelling companion, Lisa, who doesn't eat sweets at all.

P.S. Tony Hamnet – sorry we missed your party!

CONTENTS:

What's in This Book

8 Introduction

13 THE SWEET STORE CUPBOARD
23 GETTING TO GRIPS WITH SUGAR
37 THE TOOL CUPBOARD
41 SAFETY IN THE SWEET KITCHEN

45 THE GREAT BRITISH SWEETS
46 Acid Drops
48 Almond Cake
49 Aniseed Balls
51 Aniseed Sweets
52 Barley Sugar
55 Black Man
56 Bonfire Toffee
58 Butterscotch
61 Chocolate Limes
64 Chocolate Orange
65 Clove Rock
68 Cock on a Stick
70 Coconut Ice
73 Coconut Sweets
74 Coltsfoot Rock
76 Cornish Clotted Cream Fudge
77 Curly Wurly
81 Devon Double Cream Caramels
82 Edinburgh Rock
86 Everton Toffee
88 Fisherman's Friend
91 Fruit Pastilles
94 Gobstoppers
96 Hawick Balls
97 Humbugs
101 Jelly Babies

103 Kendal Mint Cake
105 Lemon Drops
106 Liquorice
110 Liquorice Allsorts
112 Loshin Du
113 Love Hearts
116 Macaroon Bars
119 Mackintosh's Special Toffee
120 Mars Bar
122 Mealie Candy
123 Nougat
125 Nutty Nubs
127 Parma Violets
129 Pear Drops
131 Peggy's Leg
133 Peppermint Creams
134 Polo Mints
135 Riley's Bridgend Toffee
139 Rock (the seaside stuff)
140 Sherbet
143 Smarties
147 Soor Plooms
148 Sugared Almonds
149 Tablet
151 Brechin Tablet
153 Taffi Triog
154 Taffi Twm
155 Tatties
157 Walnut Whip
159 Wine Gums
162 Yellow Man

168 Bibliography
170 Acknowledgements

INTRODUCTION

This Sugared Isle ...

From the North to the South and the East to the West, we British are never very far from small, sugary objects, generally sparkling with colour, often a miniature work of art, which are deeply loved yet often over-looked. Yes, I'm talking about our Great British Sweets!

Britain 'does' sweets like no other nation on earth. But why? Historically we have had easy access to sugar. During the eighteenth and nineteenth centuries Britain became one of the largest importers of sugar from the West Indies and the Americas and our consumption of the sweet stuff increased to match its availability. But it's not just about the sugar.

I'd argue that the very nature of what it is to be British has a large part – possibly the most important part – to play in our great talent for invent-ing sweets. All the imagination, ingenuity, eccentricity and – most of all – the sense of humour that are part and parcel of our psyche are essential factors in explaining why Britain leads the way in sweet-making. After all, many of our traditional sweets are made of very few ingredients – in some cases, little more than sugar and flavouring – and yet they are so much more than the sum of their parts; ingenious little pocket-money treats that we think of with such great affection. And think of the names of those sweets: gobstoppers, humbugs, claggum, Yellow Man, nutty nubs, Curly Wurly, jelly babies and flumps ... Who else but us Brits could have invented such quirky and unfathomable names for a foodstuff?

The British love affair with sweets runs deep. In a fashion that can only be considered akin to Marcel Proust and his madeleine moment, sucking or biting into a childhood favourite can give rise to a fevered rush of nostalgia, throwing some of us back to endless summers, chopper bikes, space hoppers, grazed knees, first sticky kisses and the joy of spending our own pocket money. Sweets are an important part of our culture, our history, and our pride in where we come from and I wanted to find out more about them and why they are so revered.

...

I took a map and stuck a small marker on every city, town or village that has a sweet either associated with it or named after it. Before long, much of the map was hidden under a thick sprinkling of bright pink tags. And I decided, with my friend Lisa, to hunt down the inventors and makers of these amazing sweets in order to compile a compendium of some of our greatest British sweets. The subject of confectionery in general is vast, and so it was good to define some parameters in order to be able to narrow the list and assess what would make the cut for this book.

First, the sweet had to be invented in Britain. Secondly, I looked for the sweets that had odd and unexpected stories attached (a good example of this is the humble aniseed ball – who would have considered that it would be tested as a detonation device for a limpet mine?) Thirdly, the sweets had to have withstood the test of time. I realised that the sweets invented more recently by focus groups or marketing experts just didn't hit the mark in quite the same way. The striking result of all this is that there are quite a lot of toffees in the book; all are slightly different, though, according to regional variations such as the availability of certain ingredients – the rich milk in Devon and Cornwall, or oats in Scotland.

Along the way I made some fascinating discoveries. I was surprised to notice that the sweet industry in the UK is incredibly healthy. At a time when we are constantly being told the manufacturing industry is dead, I discovered that the opposite is true, at least as far as confectionery is concerned. And not only that, but the majority of sweet-makers I encountered are actually expanding, Sweet shops, too, are on the rise.

The other exciting thing I learned was that lots of our sweet companies have been going for years and years – hundreds of years in some cases. One sweet maker, Grays of Dudley, is still going strong after five generations, with one member of the founding family describing working for the company as 'like being on board a ship, everyone working together and pitching in to do whatever needs to be done'. Sweet makers are also passionate people. I found an Indian confectioner in Scotland, Sunny Pahuja, who saved 150 jobs by investing his life savings in a sweet company that he was passionate about, and I found a young couple in Bridgend, Steve and Freya, who took on the mighty Kraft empire to rescue their famous family name – and won. I discovered that the Quaker families who founded some of our most illustrious confectionery companies were ahead of their time in treating their staff fairly and in paying women the same wages as men. I found another long-established family company who are currently re-jigging their operation to encompass the sixth generation of owners, two little boys aged just seven and ten at the time of writing, who are keen to get going in the business. What a legacy those boys will have!

Finally, it would appear that Great Britain is full of unsung sweetie heroes: people who have made a significant contribution to the sticky pantheon of British confectionery in some way, either inventing and making sweets, inventing equipment to make them, or selling sweets – or all three. Where possible, I have named these people, because they deserve recognition. You can read more about the road trips, and the people I met, on my website www.adelenozedar.com.

...

For the most part I've included a recipe for each sweet so that you can make it at home yourself, or else I have devised recipes that use the sweets themselves as an ingredient. Making your own sweets is easy and fun and makes them the proper treat they were always intended to be. It's time to shine the spotlight on one of our most unique, marvellous and magical inventions; the Great British Sweet!

Disclaimer
I apologise if I have left out your favourite sweet. I know there are bound to be some I will be kicking myself about.

THE SWEET STORE CUPBOARD:

What's in Your Sweets and Why

Whilst I've deliberately made sure that the recipes in this book don't require any rare or difficult ingredients, the following is an explanation of the main ingredients you will need and what they actually do.

SWEET-MAKING SUNDRIES

Baking powder
A combination of bicarbonate of soda plus cream of tartar, baking powder acts as a raising agent in sweets and cakes as well as reacting with boiling sugars, as explained below.

Bicarbonate of soda
Sometimes called baking soda, this is a raising agent used in baking. Now for some school chemistry. Its scientific name is 'sodium bicarbonate' and it is a 'base', which means it's the opposite of an acid substance. The scale of acidity is called the pH scale where a pH of 7 designates neutral. Anything lower is acidic and anything higher is alkaline.

When a recipe involving boiling sugar calls for a dash of bicarbonate of soda, you might notice that it's usually added towards the end of the recipe. The sugars that you are boiling are acid and the heating of sugars contributes to the acidity. Because it is alkaline, the addition of bicarbonate of soda will raise the pH balance of the sugar mixture. When the bicarbonate of soda is added at the end of the boiling process, the sugar dramatically froths up the sides of the pan very quickly as the alkaline reacts with the acid.

Citric acid
At one-time a staple of small groceries and also previously widely available in pharmacies, citric acid is now a bit harder to find on the high street. If you're lucky enough to be travelling in India, stock up on some

lovely packets of Blue Bird citric acid, since it's readily available there. Otherwise, keep your eyes peeled in independent grocery stores and chemist's shops or find it online.

As the name suggests, the acid was originally extracted from lemon juice. And because Italy has an abundance of lemons, the citric acid business was developed to an industrial scale there during the last decade of the nineteenth century. As well as acting as a preservative, citric acid prevents the crystallisation of boiling sugar and can also be used as an emulsifier, preventing the separation of fats in, say, ice cream. It also enhances flavours and adds a certain acidic tang.

Cream of tartar

Since we seem to be having a mini-science lesson here, the proper name for this common over-the-counter ingredient is potassium bitartrate. It's a weaker form of tartaric acid (see page 16). Despite the name, cream of tartar has nothing to do with dairy. In making sweets, cream of tartar prevents crystallisation in sugar.

And here's a handy tip for keen bakers: if you're whisking egg whites to stiff peaks, a pinch of cream of tartar will increase their volume as well as preventing the whites from separating.

Gelatine

Vegetarians eschew the use of gelatine, which is made from the bones of animals (generally pigs or cows) but it's the collagen content in gelatine that helps liquids to set and gives sweets a bouncy, gummy texture. Gelatine comes in various different forms, including powder or in leaves. There are vegetarian setting agents too, which work just as well if you prefer them, notably agar agar or carrageenan, both made from seaweed. If you are making jellied sweets from the juice of pineapple, papaya or kiwi fruit, be aware that gelatine will have no effect, since the enzymes in these fruits break down its protein content and the liquid will not set.

Gum arabic

This is the hardened sap of two different kinds of acacia tree, used in a wide variety of applications (including glue, shoe polish, printmaking and fireworks) and often used in sweets as a thickening agent and stabiliser as well as for its gummy texture and emulsifying properties. If you want to experiment with it, you can buy it from Indian supermarkets under the name of 'goond'.

Gum tragacanth (or just tragacanth)

Like gum arabic, tragacanth is obtained from a tree, the Astragalus gummifer, which grows in parts of the Middle East and also in Turkey. It has been in use since the seventeenth century, introduced to Europe by the French after their colonisation of North Africa. It was the itinerant French gum traders that provided yet another revolutionary development in the British sweet industry.

Fruit gums and wine gums used to be made with gum arabic. Gum tragacanth is a cheaper, more reliable substitute. It is sometimes known by the more exotic name of gum dragon. Why 'dragon'? 'Tragacanth' was frequently mispronounced as 'dragon'.

Tartaric acid

If you want to get really technical and call tartaric acid by its proper name, it's dihydroxysuccinic acid. It was originally discovered as a byproduct of the wine-making process (although it occurs naturally in some plants). Viticulturists noticed a white sediment that formed on the wine casks, a sort of salt. This 'salt' is called argol – it is used to make tartaric acid. Tartaric acid is not only harder to get hold of than cream of tartar, but is also pricier.

Vinegar

Lots of recipes for toffee call for a dash of vinegar. The addition of vinegar helps prevent the sugar from crystallising, and makes for a toffee with a smooth texture. Quite who discovered this, or when, we have no idea. Many recipes for treacle toffee call for pale vinegar but it's fine to use malt vinegar instead. You can also use fruit vinegars if you wish, although the dark balsamic kind can leave a bit of a tang – not unpleasant, just odd.

DAIRY PRODUCTS

Butter
Buy the best butter possible; the cheap stuff just isn't good enough as it doesn't have that rich, creamy flavour. Use unsalted butter unless stated otherwise. I also like to use the butter that's regional to the sweet, (i.e. Irish butter for Yellow Man) but that's just my little foible.

Condensed milk
Many people find this too cloying on its own (although my granny told me a condensed milk sandwich was a rare treat), but its sweetness and texture make it a popular choice in many sweet recipes. As with evaporated milk, some sixty per cent of the water content of the milk is removed and sugar is added. This gloopy, dense liquid is actually 40–45 per cent sugar. Condensed milk pours very slowly because it's as thick as treacle.

Cream
Cream is the liquid, rich in butter fat, that rises to the top of milk after it has been allowed to settle. Single cream contains 18 per cent fat, and can be used to replace milk in a recipe, but not the other way round. Double cream contains 48 per cent fat and is known as 'heavy cream' in the USA. The two types are not interchangeable in sweet recipes because their different texture and fat content will affect the outcome.

Evaporated milk

In the process of making evaporated milk, around 60 per cent of the water content of the milk is removed, which concentrates the natural sweetness of the milk without needing to add sugar. During the heating process, the sugars in the milk caramelise a little, hence the distinctive flavour that is useful in sweet recipes. Evaporated milk, like sweetened condensed milk, has the advantage of a long shelf life but it is much thinner than the former and has a similar pouring consistency to normal fresh milk.

Milk

The full-fat content of whole milk is the best for making sweets, giving a richer, smoother taste and a creamier texture.

CHOCOLATE

The Aztecs and Mexicans enjoyed chocolate – 'chocolatl' or 'bitter water'– for many centuries before the Spanish Conquistadores arrived in the 16th Century. It's the bean pods of the cocoa tree, or Theobroma cacao, that give us our chocolate.

Although indigenous to South America, the cacao tree now grows in lots of different parts of the world including Ghana, Malaysia, India and the Ivory Coast, which has the greatest number of them. The beans are fermented for a few days and then dried to produce 'nibs'. Chocolate is produced by blending these nibs with sugar and cocoa butter and sometimes milk.

Until chocolate became affordable in the UK, sweets in Britain were primarily about the boiling of sugar. Prior to the seventeenth century, chocolate had been a rich man's treat, available only to a wealthy few, and was used as a drink. However, the coming of the Industrial Revolution meant that, from the latter half of the 1700s, chocolate could be produced in large volumes and at a price that anyone could afford. It also meant that existing sweet manufacturers could experiment with this exciting ingredient.

A solid bar of chocolate is something we take for granted today, but it took quite a bit of trial and error before a method of forming chocolate in such a way was refined. A Quaker physician, Joseph Fry, was the first person to do this, in 1847. He blended sugar and cocoa butter into a paste meaning that a bar could be formed. These days, it takes two and a half years to become a qualified chocolatier.

The UK is going through something of a renaissance in terms of artisan chocolate, seeing an increasing number of small, bespoke producers springing up. However, for the purposes of making some of the sweets in this book, nothing more will be required of you than to melt down commercial chocolate bars. Whether you use a bain marie (a bowl suspended over simmering water) or a microwave, the point to bear in mind is not to allow any water or other liquid to come into contact with the melting chocolate, otherwise it will 'seize' and start to solidify in small lumps.

Tempering Chocolate

Once melted, cocoa butter crystallises during the cooling process and it produces crystals of varying sizes. This variance results in two chocolate disasters: a patchy dull surface on the cooled chocolate (when ideally the chocolate should be glossy) and a dry-ish, crumbly texture. 'Tempering' chocolate is the means of controlling the temperature of those crystals so that they remain evenly sized. For the most part, the recipes in this book will not require you to temper your chocolate, however, it's worth knowing what it means and how to do it.

Break your chocolate into smallish pieces and set one third aside. Place the rest of the chocolate pieces in a heatproof bowl. Heat 5cm of water in a pan and place the bowl of chocolate over the top, making sure that the bottom of the bowl is not touching the water. Allow the chocolate to melt slowly until the temperature reaches:

45–50°C for dark chocolate
40–45°C for milk chocolate
40°C for white chocolate

As soon as the temperature is reached, take the bowl off the heat. Add the remaining unmelted chocolate into the melted chocolate. Stir the chocolate together until the temperature reaches:

28–29°C for dark chocolate
27–28°C for milk chocolate
26–27°C for white chocolate

This will take 5–7 minutes, stirring all the time to get as much air as possible into the chocolate to help cool it down quicker. You can also place a small bowl of ice or cold water underneath the bowl of chocolate to help cool it down quicker.

Next, increase the temperature but only by a few degrees, taking care not to overheat. Keep a bowl of cold water close at hand and pop the bowl of melted chocolate into it to cool it down if you accidentally overheat it. Place the chocolate back over the pan on low heat until the temperature reaches:

31–32°C for dark chocolate
29–30°C for milk chocolate
28–29°C for white chocolate

Your chocolate is now tempered and ready to use.

GETTING TO GRIPS WITH SUGAR:

How it Works and Why

As the key ingredient in sweet-making, your cupboard will be filled with bags of sugar of all different types and textures. But before you embark on your culinary endeavours, getting to grips with what sugar is and how it works will really help you to understand the processes involved in sweet-making and ultimately ensure you're more likely to get the results you want. So this section offers a little insight into the mysteries and magic of sugar and how to handle it well.

TYPES OF SUGAR

After sugar is initially processed from the sugar cane, there are two end products: the rich, dark, moist molasses, and a dark brown raw sugar.

The raw sugar is refined to make a golden granulated sugar, which can then be further processed to make white sugars. This kind of sugar is often called for in sweet-making because it has a 'neutral' taste.

The colour and type of raw sugar depends on how much molasses has been removed. Types of raw sugars include demerara, light and dark muscovado sugar and molasses sugar. These sugars have a delicious, complex flavour. The very brittle demerara will take a longer time to dissolve than the moist muscovado.

The range of refined white sugars, from the finest to the chunkiest, is as follows.

Icing sugar (also called confectioners' sugar) is virtually a powder, which, provided you sift it properly, results in a smooth texture when mixed with water or juice. It's often used in recipes that don't require cooking.

Caster sugar is a fine sugar that is good for sweet-making because it melts quickly. However, if the recipe calls specifically for caster sugar and you only have granulated, you can pulverise the granulated sugar with a blender.

Granulated sugar is the next size up in terms of granule. It also has a low melting point and dissolves easily.

Preserving sugar has added pectin, which helps jams and jellies to set. Pectin occurs naturally in apples.

Incidentally, if you have old-fashioned recipe books, you might see references to 'loaf sugar'; this was a cone-shaped solid block of refined sugar, available until the end of the nineteenth century when it was replaced with cube sugar (made from sugar crystals and sugar syrup, poured into moulds and dried – an efficient way of packaging sugar).

If you have an Indian supermarket in the vicinity, you can buy Jaggery, which is made from a mix of sugar cane and the sap of the date palm tree, in a similar form.

Sugar is comprised of two simple sugars, fructose and glucose, glued together. An acid ingredient – such as citric acid or tartaric acid – will split these two components. When this happens, the process is called 'inversion' ... that's what it means when packaging lists 'invert sugars'.

HOW SUGAR WORKS

When you heat sugar and water, the heat causes the sugar crystals to dissolve, making a sugar solution. When as much sugar as possible has been dissolved in the water, then the solution is called 'saturated'. The higher the temperature, the greater the amount of sugar can be dissolved in the water. At very high temperatures (such as the ones involved in sweet making) virtually all the water will have evaporated, but the sugar remains in a solution. However, when the mixture starts to cool, it means that there is more sugar held in solution than would normally be possible; the term for this is 'supersaturation'. Supersaturation is an unstable state and as such the sugar crystals will want to revert to a solid state, through crystallisation. Any movement (such as knocking the pan) will cause this to happen, making sugar molecules lock together like pieces of a jigsaw. Depending on the sort of sweets you are making, you might desire this crystallisation (as in fudge) or you might want to avoid it (smooth-textured sweets, like toffees).

Crystallisation is prevented by the addition of a further simple sugar, such as fructose or glucose. This is because the existing sugar crystals are all uniform in shape and lock together. The incoming fructose or glucose has molecules of a different shape and size and so gets in the way of the ones trying to cluster together. Golden syrup performs this action very well, hence its use in many recipes.

Crystallisation can also be prevented by adding an acid to the mix. This is where the addition of ingredients such as cream of tartar or citric acid suddenly makes sense.

A good example of sugar crystallising are those sticks with pretty clusters of sugar crystals coating the end, which are used to stir fancy coffee in fancy places by fancy people. The technical term for this sweet is rock candy. It's not at all tricky to make it at home and it is a good way to learn and see how sugar works.

Rock Candy

250ml water
500–750g white granulated sugar, plus a further ½ tablespoon
liquid or powder food colouring (optional)

a wooden skewer or a clean, plain wooden chopstick
a clothes peg
a tall, narrow, heatproof glass container, slim enough for the clothes peg to lie across the top (a heatproof vase or tumbler will do the job)

Clip the clothes peg to the skewer in such a way that the skewer will hang to about 3cm from the bottom of the glass container. Take the skewer out of the container.

In a heavy-bottomed pan, bring the water to the boil. Add a couple of drops/pinches of the food colouring if you're using it.

Tip about 100g of the sugar into the boiling water and let it dissolve, stirring all the while. Then keep adding the sugar to the water, 100g at a time, stirring to dissolve each batch thoroughly otherwise the experiment won't work (a little patience is required!). Keep adding sugar until you've reached supersaturation point – you'll know you've reached it because no more sugar will dissolve, then take the pan off the stove and allow it to cool for 20 minutes.

Take the skewer, dip half of it in the sugar solution in the pan, roll it in the half tablespoonful of sugar, and allow it to cool completely by hanging it in a dry place over a bowl to catch any drips. This helps to kick-start the formation of crystals.

Carefully pour the liquid – which will still be hot – into the glass container. Put the sugared skewer into the glass, using the peg to suspend it to the position you checked earlier. Make sure that the skewer isn't touching the sides of the container.

When the container has cooled (about an hour depending on the ambient temperature), put it somewhere that it won't be disturbed for the next week. Put a piece of foil loosely over the top to keep it dust-free, then just wait for those beautiful sugar crystals to form. This will take 2–3 days, but again, be patient. It can take as long as a week to see the result of your labours!

COOKING WITH SUGAR

Nothing is more magical than creating something sweet and beautiful from a bit of simple, everyday sugar. Sugar work is complicated, however, and requires precision so it's useful to have a few general tips on how to work with sugar in order to ensure success.

Always use a sturdy heavy-bottomed saucepan (see p.38) and heat the sugar and other ingredients over low heat, stirring from time to time, until the sugar is dissolved.

Only bring the sugar mixture to the boil once the sugar has dissolved/melted. This will help avoid crystallisation which can occur if there are undissolved grains of sugar in the mixture.

Always use clean wooden spoons.

Do not stir the mixture once it has begun to boil unless specifically instructed to do so in the recipe.

Wash down the inside edges of the pan with a clean pastry brush dipped in water to rinse of any crystals that form above the boiling sugar. This will help prevent possible crystallisation.

Skim off and discard any scum that forms on the surface of the boiling sugar.

Take extra care when working with hot sugar. Sugar burns are very nasty. Keep your work area clear and uncluttered and avoid dangling clothing, hair and jewellery.

When making sweets temperature is critical so it's important to invest in a sugar thermometer (they don't cost much). There are two types of thermometers available. One is a glass thermometer in a metal frame which keeps the glass from touching the bottom of the pan. The readings are printed on the side of the metal frame. The other type has a pointed metal shaft with a gauge at the top end. When using a sugar thermometer with a metal shaft ensure that the end does not touch the base of the pan.

When using a sugar thermometer, clip it to the inside of the pan at the start of cooking so that its temperature matches that of the ingredients.

In order to get an accurate reading from sugar thermometers it is vital that the boiling liquid comes at least halfway up the shaft of the thermometer or amply covers the bulb of a glass thermometer. If there is not enough liquid in the pan to get an accurate reading you might have to carefully tip the pan.

Always read the temperature without removing the thermometer from the liquid, otherwise it won't be accurate.

Sugar turns liquid at 100°C. Once it starts getting hotter than that, the fun begins. In the old days, before the sugar thermometer became widely available in the nineteenth century, sugar boilers would simply lick their finger and stick it into the liquid to test for 'low' temperatures that would have been in the area of 100°C. Higher temperatures required a more careful approach and although confectioners even today refer to their 'asbestos hands', sugar burns are not to be risked. Whilst the accuracy of your sugar thermometer will make it an essential part of your kit, you could also use the old-fashioned methods of testing for a set and gauging the temperature of your sugar. This method takes a little practice, and is not as exact as a thermometer, but it is very useful to be familiar with the different stages. (The cold water test for sugar syrups is also a handy way of checking if your thermometer is working properly.)

All you'll need is a bowl of very cold water close to the stove and due care and attention. During the cooking stage, remove your pan from the heat and drop a small spoonful of sugar syrup into the cold water. According to the shape and texture of the resulting sugar ball, you can determine the approximate temperature of your sugar. Note that there is quite a range in temperature for each stage, so follow the temperature in the recipe for the best results. The names for the different stages are accurately descriptive.

Thread (102–113°C)

This stage isn't used very often in making sweets, but it's a useful test when making syrups, preserves, fruit liqueurs and some icings. If you scoop some of the thin syrup on to a spoon, it will pour straight off in a fine thread into the cold water. If you leave it on the spoon, it will thicken slightly and pucker a little when you pinch it, and brittle threads will form between your finger and thumb, hence the name.

Pearl (104–106°C)

The thread formed by pulling the liquid sugar can be stretched. When a small dollop is plopped into cold water, the sugar forms soft little pearl-like balls.

Soft Ball (113–116°C)

If you drip some of the thickening syrup into the cold water, you can then pick up the goo and roll it into a soft ball. This is the temperature you'll be aiming for when you're making fudge, fondant and Turkish Delight, for example.

Firm Ball (118–121°C)

Dip your hand into the water and form the sugar into a small ball. When out of the water the ball should be sticky and pliable but hold its shape. Sugar boilers and their apprentices would have had fun at this stage – and so can you – because a small ball of the stuff will bounce off any hard surface: floor, ceiling, windows.

Hard Ball (121–130°C)

The sugar syrup should easily form a ball in the cold water and if removed from the water will hold its shape and be sticky but rigid. This is the stage to be reached when making marshmallow, nougat and some toffees.

Soft Crack (132–143°C)

Dropped into the cold water, the syrup immediately sets, and cracks if you chew it, sticking to your teeth. This is the desired stage when making Edinburgh Rock and hard toffee.

Hard Crack (149–154°C)

Once removed from the water, the syrup will have become solid, very brittle with a glassy snappiness and no longer sticky to touch. This is the temperature required for boiled sweets.

Light Caramel (160–170°C)

At this stage, the sugar mixture starts to change colour, darkening rapidly. This process is called caramelisation. Light caramel should be a pale honey colour and is the stage when making pralines.

Caramel (up to 177°C)

The sugar syrup will have turned a lovely deep amber in colour. Be careful; it's easy for the mixture to boil too high and become too dark. The temperature at which the sugar will have 'gone over' is at the highest point mentioned but you really won't need a thermometer to tell you that your sugar is burned!

A word of warning: as the temperature slowly rises, it's easy to become complacent and think you can take your eye off the glass and do something else. In my experience, this is foolhardy. No sooner does your attention wander than the temperature will mysteriously soar, resulting in spoiled sweets and swear words.

PULLED SUGAR TECHNIQUE

Most boiled sweets and pulled toffees or taffies start with a combination of sugar and water, heated together to a certain temperature, to form a syrup. According to the type of sweet you are making, various flavourings, colourings or extra ingredients are then added to the basic syrup, which can then be handled in different ways as it cools – pulled, stretched and manipulated, or simply poured into a mould. Each has surprisingly different end results. For example, if you simply pour the liquid into a mould the result will be a smooth, glossy, hard sweet. If you decide to manipulate the sugar by pulling and stretching it, the resulting aeration will be an opaque sweet with a silky texture. As you pull and stretch, the colour will lighten.

Below is a basic pulled sweet recipe to which you can add whatever flavourings or colourings the recipe calls for. It's really worth having a go at this before you attempt some of the other recipes in the book so you can get used to pulling, twisting and shaping the lovely pliable boiled sugar before you get cracking on more complicated sweets.

Pulled toffee, or 'taffie'

400g caster sugar
100ml liquid glucose
100ml water
flavourings or colourings of your
  choice (optional)

38cm x 30cm shallow baking tray,
  buttered

Pre-heat the oven to 100°C/gas mark ¼.

Place all the ingredients in a heavy-bottomed pan, attach your sugar thermometer to the inside of the pan, making sure that the bottom of it is immersed in the ingredients, then place the pan over a low heat. Stir until everything is melted together, then turn up the heat. Don't stir for this next part.

Allow the mixture to come to the boil and, keeping a close eye on the thermometer, remove from the heat the second it reaches the temperature specified in the recipe – in this case, 143°C ('soft crack' stage).

Leave the mixture for five minutes before you add any flavourings, otherwise the flavour will simply evaporate in the heat. Pour the molten substance into your buttered tray or on to an oiled surface and leave for a few minutes. You'll see that a skin forms on top of the toffee and if you dab gingerly at the edges it will shrink from the sides easily.

Once it is just about cool enough to handle, practise scooping the toffee repeatedly into the centre with an oiled metal scraper or spatula, allowing it to ooze out again at the sides. This will take up to 10 minutes depending on the ambient temperature. Soon you'll be able to pick up chunks of it safely. So long as the toffee remains warm, you can handle it, and you can even pop it back into a warm oven for a few minutes to keep it pliable. As practice, take a fist-sized chunk (leaving the rest in the oven). Oil your hands, as well as the work surface, so that the toffee doesn't stick to them. Then start to stretch and pull it, and as you do so the toffee will become creamy and smooth with a satiny sheen. This will happen faster as you get the hang of it, and should eventually take no more than a couple of minutes. Pretend it's plasticine and practise pulling it into a long rope, then twisting back on itself and shaping it. Don't try to work it if it starts to 'set' otherwise it will crack and crumble. Pop in the warm oven to reconstitute, as above. It's great fun for children!

Fondant

Classic sugar fondant, from the French verb fondre, *'to melt', is a thick paste made out of a sugar syrup heated to soft ball stage and then worked when cool to form a smooth, pliant white paste.*

Here is a quicker and easier recipe for a fondant that requires no cooking, handy for making simple sweets like sugar mice, truffles, and flavoured 'creams' (such as mint or violet). This sugar fondant recipe is simple to make, although it does need some elbow grease if you don't have an electric mixer.

450g icing sugar, sifted
2 medium egg whites
½ tbsp lemon juice

2-3 of drops of flavouring and colouring (optional)

Simply mix the ingredients together well until you have a smooth, base fondant. You may need to add a little extra water if the mixture is too stiff to shape easily.

STORING SWEETS

Wrap in greaseproof paper and store in airtight jars or tins in a cool place. Toffee wrapped in waxed paper will last for two weeks in an airtight container. Boiled sweets, wrapped individually and stored in an airtight container, can last for months. Any sweets with a high dairy content, such as chocolate cream truffles, need to be refrigerated or frozen. Packed in layers of greaseproof paper in a sealed tub and kept in the fridge they should keep for a fortnight; in the freezer, they will last at least a month. Dairy fudge stored the same way will be good for three weeks, or for up to three months if frozen.

THE TOOL CUPBOARD:

What You Need to Make Sweets and Why

EQUIPMENT

It's likely that you will be able to piece together the bits and pieces you need for making sweets at home, even if you have only an averagely togged-up kitchen. However, I'd recommend the following essentials.

A good heavy-bottomed saucepan

This is an absolute must, and if you don't have a suitable one, it's important to invest in one. Remember, if you develop a real taste for sweet making, this pan will become your best friend. The sides of the pan must be high enough to allow for the safe bubbling of molten sugar (see page 28), and the base has to be wide enough to ensure the contents don't catch and burn. My favourite pan is 20cm high by 24cm wide. The base also needs to be flat, not wobbly or dented. And if you get really enthusiastic you might add a gorgeous proper copper pan to your Christmas list. Copper pans are still used by professional sweet makers and ensure an even distribution of heat, essential when dealing with scalding materials.

Sugar Thermometer

This is another essential, since accurate measurement of temperatures can mean the difference between success and failure.

Generally, sugar thermometers clip to the side of your pan so you have both hands free to stir and pour. You need to bring the thermometer and the ingredients of the pan up to heat at the same time; you should never plonk a cold thermometer directly into a hot substance, otherwise the glass might break.

Good-quality large baking trays and baking tins

Some of the recipes in this book call for a 'large baking tray' to be used as a work surface. You'll need a tray that is at least 38 x 30cm; larger is also fine.

Wooden spoons and spatulas

These are vital as they don't conduct the heat. Choose ones with long handles.

Work surface

You need an appropriate surface on which to scrape, fold, pull, twist and generally handle toffee. The traditional material for this used to be marble, since it provides a cool, flat surface. If you can get hold of a decent-sized chunk of marble (from a salvage merchant) it will prove invaluable. Otherwise, a large, chunky metal tray of the type used by professional caterers will do the job. Wooden boards are no good; the toffee will stick to them and they are a nightmare to clean.

Scraper or palette knife

For scooping and folding molten sugar, a wide metal or silicone palette knife will do fine, or a (clean) wallpaper scraper.

You'll also need

a selection of bowls (heatproof and otherwise)
weighing scales
a ladle (for pouring liquid into moulds)
sweet moulds (if you want to make shaped sweets)
a good pair of scissors
knives
a fat brush (useful for brushing toffee from the insides of the pan)
strainers and sieves
a wire balloon whisk and an electric whisk
greaseproof paper and wrapping materials

A note on washing up: Washing out pans and equipment that has hardened sugar stuck to it is easy enough; hot water will melt it away.

SAFETY IN THE SWEET KITCHEN: What to Look out for and Why

Apart from a few recipes, which require little or no cooking, for the most part you will be dealing with high temperatures and scalding-hot molten sugar. Many professional sweet makers treat blisters and burns as an occupational hazard – however, there's no need for you to suffer in this way.

Make sure that all pan handles are secure and not loose, and that work surfaces are clear.

Arrange all equipment so that you will be making the shortest journey possible between your stove and the work surface that you will be pouring the hot liquid on to.

Ensure that your pan is not too heavy for one person to lift safely.

Keep some burns ointment to hand, just in case.

Author's Note

The recipes in this book have been tested by me, so you have the benefit of my many mistakes. Follow the recipes to the letter and you will, for the most part, have good results though some might need a bit of practice to get them perfect. Bear in mind that mistakes frequently result in the best sweets of all; be kind to the ones that go wrong. Just give them a different name and serve them up anyway. You can't go far wrong with burnt toffee, for example, smashed up and added to ice cream.

Where it has been possible to tell you exactly how many squares or pieces of confectionery you will make or how many a recipe will serve, I have done so. But the sizes you make will vary so in the main you'll find it's up to you how many you make. And sweets that require being broken or smashed are a different matter entirely!

And finally ...

There's an extra ingredient in all cooking, I am convinced, which is impossible to buy. Without exception, the many sweet makers I met whilst writing this book were inordinately jolly and cheerful people. Given that thoughts are powerful things, it struck me that this positive attitude must rub off on the products themselves. So, when you are sifting and stirring and scorching, keep happy thoughts in your head and see if that feeling doesn't affect what you're making.

THE GREAT BRITISH SWEETS:

How to Make them at Home

ACID DROPS

Sour sweets have always been popular, in one form or another. These punk rockers of the sweet counter hold a gleeful appeal to children; in particular, those neon-coloured, chemically-enhanced sweets that they dare one another to slurp up or spray on the tongue (Toxic Waste, Vicious Vipers and Eye Poppers). But sweets that make your eyes water and your tongue shrivel in pain are nothing new. The appropriately-named 'acid drops' – the lurid lime or lemon-coloured ovals, sour enough to make your mouth turn inside out – are a good example. They're mentioned in Aurelia, a comic poem by Samuel Hoole, published in 1783: '... Smooth comfits, acid drops, and creams of ice ...'. And there's a recipe dated some 60-odd years later in The Complete Confectioner, Pastry-cook and Baker: Plain and Practical *by Eleanor Parkinson. This method isn't actually that dissimilar to the 1844 recipe of Eleanor's.*

450g granulated sugar
150ml water
7–10g tartaric acid (to taste)
2 drops lime green food colouring
  (optional)

icing sugar, for dusting
  (optional)

20 x 30cm baking tin, oiled

Preheat the oven to 100°C/gas mark ¼.

Stir the sugar and water in a heavy-bottomed saucepan, clip your sugar thermometer to the inside of the pan, place the pan over a moderate heat until the sugar is dissolved. Bring to the boil and boil steadily until the mixture reaches 156°C (hard crack stage), then remove from the heat immediately.

Allow the mixture to cool slightly, then add the tartaric acid and stir thoroughly. The more tartaric acid you add, the tarter the sweet.

ACID DROPS

Pour the mixture into the oiled tin, then cut into 1cm-wide strips as soon as the mixture is cool enough to handle. Cut these into 2cm-long strips with oiled scissors then roll into balls and leave them to set (you could make bigger acid drops if you prefer). The edges of the mixture cool first, so work from the outside in. You can also use a warm oven to keep the mixture soft whilst rolling the balls. If you fancy, dust the acid drop balls with icing sugar as they cool. Prepare for your tongue to shrivel and your face to turn inside out.

ALMOND CAKE
Scotland

The name of this recipe is deceptive for it's not a 'cake' at all, but a rich, nutty, toffee bar flavoured with lemon. It's a Scottish confection that dates back to at least the early part of the eighteenth century and I came across the recipe in a historical account of all sorts of Scottish food and customs – The Scots Kitchen by F. Marian McNeill, first published in 1929. Note that I've stayed true to the original measurements so you'll need to dust off a proper china teacup before you get going.

4 teacups caster sugar
3 tbsp golden syrup
1¼ teacups water
lump of butter the size of a
   hen's egg

150g blanched almonds
   (in halves)
zest of 1 lemon

32 x 22cm baking tray,
   buttered

Put the blanched almond halves into the tray. Then into a large heavy-bottomed pan, put the sugar, syrup and water. Bring to a rolling boil, cook for 10 minutes before adding the butter. Boil again until the mixture starts to harden. Add the lemon zest. Then pour the toffee over the nuts, leave to cool a little and score deep grooves to make bars (or chunks if you prefer).

ANISEED BALLS

I love Edith Nesbit, especially The Story of the Treasure Seekers, *and was re-reading it recently. I was thrilled to find that there's a mention of aniseed balls in the book, which proves they've been around at least since it was published in 1899. The children in the book, Dora, Dick, Oswald, Alice and Noel decide they might make a fortune if they can invent a medicine against that most tedious yet tenacious of ailments, the common cold. Among the ingredients that Oswald buys to try to make the potion there is 'a pennyworth of alum, because it is so cheap, and some turpentine, which everyone knows is good for colds, and a little sugar and an aniseed ball …'. Sadly, the medicine didn't work.*

It's understandable that the children would have used aniseed because its fresh flavour does clear the nasal passages. But I found an even stranger and more unexpected use of this wonderful sweet. The great British aniseed ball – a hard, round red sweet, strongly flavoured with aniseed – made a significant contribution to the war effort in the 1940s. Just before the start of the Second World War, Major C.V Clarke experimented with aniseed balls in the making of a delay fuse for limpet mines. Designed to be attached to the underside of a ship, limpet mines were curved to make sure they fitted closely. Powerful magnets attached the mine to the ship but the tricky part was to devise a method of detonation slow enough to allow the diver, who had attached the mine, to make his escape before the blast. The limpet mine itself had been the brainchild of a gentleman called Stuart Macrae, and he and Major Clarke discovered that aniseed balls have a consistent dissolving time in

ANISEED BALLS

water and could be used to delay the detonation. The pair stripped Bedford's sweetshops of all their aniseed balls, then they drilled holes into the balls and installed tiny detonators into each one. The sweets were then tested in the swimming pool of the Bedford Modern High School, which was thankfully closed to the public for a couple of hours every time it was needed for testing.

Incidentally, a letter written by a Mr G.D Bateman to the New Scientist of 7th April 1983 reports that the aniseed ball itself needed to be protected whilst the bomb was in the hands of the diver, lest it dissolve too quickly. Although a custom-built 'plug' was eventually developed, prior to this a contraceptive sheath was used. This meant that the inventive developers bought up every single condom for miles around, which gave them something of a racy and athletic reputation.

Traditional aniseed balls require specialist equipment that is beyond the range of the domestic kitchen. Instead, here's a recipe for a more user-friendly aniseed confection.

ANISEED SWEETS

225g granulated or caster sugar   pinch of cream of tartar
75ml water   ½ tsp aniseed oil
25g butter

Put all the ingredients except the aniseed oil into a heavy-bottomed saucepan. Attach your sugar thermometer to the inside of the pan. Place over a low heat and stir until the sugar has dissolved, then turn up the heat and bring to a rolling boil until the temperature reads 143°C (soft crack stage). Skim off and discard any scum that forms on the surface of the boiling sugar. Take the pan off the heat and allow to cool for 5 minutes before stirring in the aniseed oil.

Pour the mixture on to an oiled surface and, when cool enough to handle, knead the mixture until pliable, then break off segments and roll into balls. Leave to harden in a cool place and store in an airtight jar.

BARLEY SUGAR

This is a sweet that, despite being not a whole lot more than a boiled sugar recipe with some added colourings, is still thought of as being somehow 'good' for you. Barley sugars are glassy-looking sticks, about 15cm long. Traditionally, they were fashioned into twists and became so popular that the shape also made it into carpentry's vernacular to describe the shape of twisty chair legs, stair posts and candlesticks.

Over 300 years ago, barley sugar was actually made with barley. There's a recipe in English Housewifry by Elizabeth Moxon, published in 1764, in which barley is used. However, another recipe by Frederick Nutt in his The Compleat Confectioner dated just 25 years later doesn't call for barley at all, and simply relies on caramelisation to achieve the flavour. If you are lucky enough to find it, barley sugar made with actual barley has a distinctive, slightly malty taste. Last time I was in my local pharmacy they had a jar of barley sugar on the counter. I checked, but there was no mention of barley in the list of ingredients at all.

Predating Elizabeth Moxon's recipe by a few decades is one from an order of Benedictine Monks, dated 1638, who lived at Moret-sur-Loing in France. The monks did not have the first recipe for barley sugar and are not credited with inventing it, however their particular recipe is still in production. Indeed, the town is famous for the confection and even hosts a museum dedicated to the stuff. Sadly, because the recipe is a strictly-guarded secret, I can't tell you whether it contains any actual barley.

Barley water is famously the tipple of choice of tennis players at Wimbledon to assuage a raging thirst; this is because the barley itself

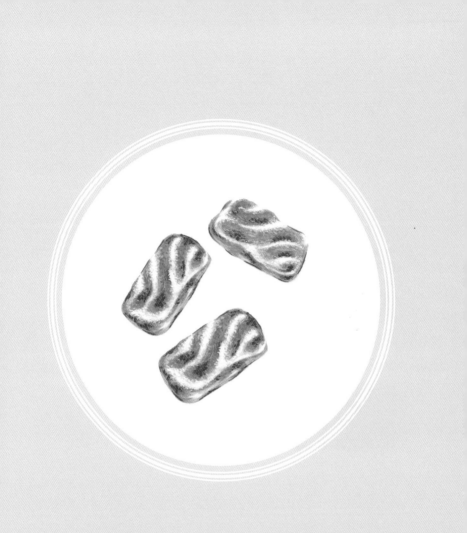

BARLEY SUGAR

has 'cooling' properties and is effective against dehydration. This might explain why it was added to sugar and sold as a health-giving confection in the first place. Incidentally, barley is also an old-fashioned remedy against heartburn, tummy ache, and diarrhoea.

Today, most commercially available barley sugar won't have been within a mile of a grain of barley, but you can make proper barley sugar very easily in your own kitchen.

Makes 20 sticks

50g pearl barley	32 x 22cm shallow baking tin, also
800ml water (or more)	buttered or oiled (if you want to
500g granulated sugar	make sweets) or a large slab,
2tsp golden syrup or liquid glucose	buttered or oiled, (if you want to
	make the traditional barley sugar
	twists)

Pour 350ml water into your pan and make a mental note of the level in the pan. Add the barley then top up with a further 250–300ml water. Bring the liquid to a simmer and simmer gently, covered, for about 1½ hours, topping up with water as necessary so that there is always at least 350ml liquid in the pan. Strain and reserve the barley water, leave to stand for about 15 minutes, so that the starchy part of the water settles to the bottom of the pan, then ladle 300ml of the clear liquid into a fresh, heavy-bottomed and high-sided pan.

Add the sugar and golden syrup or glucose to the barley water, clip your sugar thermometer to the inside of the pan and stir over a low heat until the sugar has dissolved. Bring to the boil (the mixture will foam up, hence the high-sided pan). Heat the mixture to 154°C (hard crack stage), then immediately take off the heat.

Allow the mixture to cool a little then either pour into the tin and mark into squares when just set (after about 15 minutes), or pour on to the slab and practise your pulled toffee technique (see page 32) to make twisted sticks approximately 1cm thick. After 20 minutes the sticks should be hard. Wrap in cellophane for the authentic old-fashioned 'apothecaries' counter' style.

BLACK MAN

In a word, this crunchy toffee is a Scottish version of Northern Ireland's Yellow Man toffee (see page 162). Imagine the same sort of stuff that's the inside of a Crunchie bar except give it a rich dark brown colour and you've got black man. I was really pleased to find this recipe tucked away in F. Marian McNeill's seminal work on Scottish cookery The Scots Kitchen, *which was first published in 1929. I think there should be a revival of this particular toffee since I've never seen it for sale, not even in its country of origin. Black man's honeycomb texture elevates it above the more workaday treacle toffee and I think that if I were living in Scotland I'd start my own little kitchen industry. It's worth making in quantity as gifts, but you can make less by halving or even quartering the measurements.*

250g demerara sugar
40g butter
3 tbsp black treacle

3 tbsp water
6 drops malt vinegar
1.5 level tsps bicarbonate of soda

Put everything except the vinegar and bicarbonate of soda into a deep, heavy-bottomed pan. Clip your sugar thermometer to the inside of the pan and, stirring, cook over a medium heat until the sugar dissolves. Bring to the boil and boil quickly until the thermometer reads 143°C (soft crack stage), stir in the vinegar, remove from the heat and immediately add the bicarbonate of soda. At this point the mixture will rapidly froth up the sides of the pan. Pour into a 20cm x 20cm x 5cm tray and leave to set – don't knock the sides or the bubbles will burst!

BONFIRE TOFFEE

Bonfire toffee is just one name for the treacle toffee that proliferates in many parts of the UK, albeit under different names. It's known as clag-gum, clag or clack in Scotland and the Borders, and tom trot or plot toffee (because of the Gunpowder Plot) in Yorkshire. In Wales, it's called Loshin Du. Essentially it's a hard, brittle toffee with a rich caramel flavour of black treacle, which is served smashed into pieces. Why it should be associated with the time of year around Hallowe'en and Bonfire Night, in particular, is hard to tell, although it is very comforting on a cold dark November night. At one time, all the different ways of using treacle to make toffee in the UK were a point of local pride, each of them developed in different ways, which is why I've decided to include more than one recipe in this book. The recipe for Welsh treacle toffee, Loshin Du (see page 112), for example, is very simple, whereas the one shown here is a tad more complicated in that it has more ingredients.

450g soft dark brown sugar
110g black treacle
110g golden syrup
140ml water
80g unsalted butter
1 tsp pale malt vinegar
a large pinch of ground ginger,

chilli powder or cayenne pepper, or another spice of your choice, to taste

32 x 22cm baking tray, buttered
toffee hammer (optional)

BONFIRE TOFFEE

Put all the ingredients except the spice into a heavy-bottomed pan with a lid. Fill a sink or have to hand a heatproof bowl of cold water large enough for the pan to sit inside.

Place the pan over a low heat, clip your sugar thermometer to the inside of the pan and heat until the butter has melted. Increase the heat and quickly bring to the boil. Cover and boil for 2 minutes, then uncover the pan. When the temperature has reached 143°C, (soft crack stage), remove from the heat and quickly place the pan in the cold water to stop the cooking.

If you want to add spice, now is the time. Stir it in thoroughly then pour the toffee into the tin, leave to harden, and then break into shards with a hammer or toffee hammer, if you have one.

BUTTERSCOTCH
Doncaster

Butterscotch is a type of toffee that contains a higher percentage of butter than other toffees and is generally cooked until brittle. You would be forgiven for thinking that it came from Scotland, but 'to scotch' is actually a Yorkshire term meaning 'to cut' or 'to slit'. Although the name was coined and the sweet commercialised by confectioner Samuel Parkinson in Doncaster, Yorkshire, in 1817, butterscotch had been in existence for many years before Samuel made it popular.

Confectioner's confectioner, E. Skuse, writing in his classic The Confectioners' Hand-Book and Practical Guide to the Art of Sugar Boiling *in the late nineteenth century, pointed out that Samuel Parkinson's butterscotch had very little to differentiate it from Everton toffee (see page 86). The only difference, said Skuse, was in the shape. Butterscotch was*

BUTTERSCOTCH
Doncaster

cut into small, regular pieces, rather than shattered into irregular shards with a hammer, and sold at a significantly higher price. Indeed, those slim and dainty rectangles are still an indicator that what you are eating is butterscotch. Parkinson used a specially bladed roller to slice the butterscotch into those classy, uniform pieces, which he then sold from his shop, Capo, on Doncaster's High Street.

By the middle of the nineteenth century the names of Parkinson, Doncaster and butterscotch were synonymous. By this time, too, other companies in Doncaster, including Booths and Henry Hall, had jumped on the butterscotch bandwagon and were making the sweet, although 'butterscotch' was acknowledged as the invention of Samuel Parkinson himself. What's more, Parkinson conclusively underlined his status as the boldly alliterative Britain's Best Butterscotch Baron when in 1851 it was his brand that was presented to Queen Victoria when she visited Doncaster racecourse to open the St Leger horse races. The Queen liked it so much that she placed an order with its manufacturer. After this Parkinson's Butterscotch became a significant part of St Leger, sold at the racecourse itself on race days and in shops in the town all year round.

After changing hands in 1893 and then becoming a limited company in 1912, Parkinson's Doncaster butterscotch was sold once more in 1961. Just 16 years later, though, the company was closed down. It was later revived by the Parkinson family in 2003, but sadly the doors slammed resoundingly shut on what had been the world's most famous butterscotch factory when it went into administration in 2010.

Butterscotch is not difficult to make, but it is important to stir the mixture whilst it is cooking so that it doesn't burn, especially if you are using cream, which tends to scorch at high temperatures.

450g granulated sugar or demerara sugar
100g unsalted butter
150ml double cream or milk
a pinch of cream of tartar

1 tsp vanilla essence (optional)

32 x 22cm shallow baking tin, buttered
toffee hammer (optional)

Put all the ingredients except the vanilla essence into a heavy-bottomed pan, clip your sugar thermometer to the inside and stir gently over a low heat until the sugar has dissolved. Gradually bring to the boil, stirring all the while to avoid burning, until your sugar thermometer registers a temperature of 140°C (soft crack stage). Immediately remove the pan from the heat, stir in the vanilla essence and pour into the tin.

Once it has set enough to hold, which will take no more than 10 minutes, score it into the rectangles with a knife. If you want to be very precise about this, you'll need to use a ruler to mark out the traditional size, which is 3 x 1cm, to make 96 pieces. Otherwise just go mad with your toffee hammer once the butterscotch is set.

CHOCOLATE LIMES

We know that Halls, more popularly known for their cough sweets, were making chocolate limes at the end of the nineteenth century, but what's not clear is whether Halls invented them. In fact, we don't know a whole lot about chocolate limes, apart from the fact that they are a classic British sweet – a hard, lime-flavoured sugar shell encasing a soft, slightly powdery-tasting chocolate. When you think about it, chocolate and lime is quite a sophisticated taste combination and whoever invented them must have thought that he or she had made a revolutionary breakthrough for sweet manufacturers. What's more the sweet itself has an elaborate construction. Its discoverer must have been a pretty radical sort of person.

It would be very tricky to make chocolate limes in your own home kitchen but why not give these chocolate lime truffles a try instead?

CHOCOLATE LIMES

Makes about 30 truffles

100ml double cream
finely grated zest of 1 unwaxed
    lime
400g white chocolate, broken into
    pieces

50g unsalted butter, at room
    temperature, cut into small cubes
3 drops lime extract or a splosh of
    lime liqueur
300g dark chocolate, at least 70
    per cent cocoa solids

Put the cream and the lime zest into a saucepan and bring to the boil. Take off the heat and add the white chocolate. Once the chocolate has melted put the mixture into a bowl and add the butter, then leave to cool. Once cool, add the lime extract. Beat with a wooden spoon until the mixture is smooth and creamy, then refrigerate for about an hour.

Take teaspoonfuls of the mixture and roll it into balls. Freeze overnight in a lidded plastic container with a sheet of greaseproof paper between each layer of truffles.

The next day, place a heatproof bowl over a pan of simmering water, making sure the base of the bowl isn't touching the water. Have ready a sheet of greaseproof paper near the pan. Melt the dark chocolate in the bowl, turn off the heat, then, using two forks, dip each frozen ball into the melted chocolate. Allow the excess chocolate to drip away before carefully placing each truffle on the greaseproof paper to set, which will take about 10 minutes. Stored in a tub in the refrigerator, the truffles will keep for 2 weeks, or you can freeze them for up to a month.

CHOCOLATE ORANGE
York

As seasonal as falling leaves and crackling bonfires, the Terry's Chocolate Orange is as much a part of Christmas as stockings, Santa, and … well, sweets. The beloved chocolate confection is a segmented orange shape. Tap the 'orange' on its base to release the segments.

But did you know that, before the Terry's Chocolate Orange there was a Terry's Chocolate Apple? Now there's a flavour combination that must have puckered the cheeks. The chocolate apple appeared in the 1920s and lasted until 1954. The orange, launched in the 1930s, eventually proved a much bigger hit, superseding the apple.

It would be both time-consuming and difficult, requiring specialised moulds, to try to reproduce an actual chocolate orange at home. However, you can still enjoy that lovely combination of flavours by using a chocolate orange as the basis of a delicious dessert. My particular favourite is the chocolate orange with popping candy, which is why I've used it as inspiration for the following pudding.

Chocolate Orange Bread and Butter Pudding

Serves 6–8

8 chunky slices of brioche, cut into triangles
400ml double cream
85g unsalted butter
150g dark chocolate, at least 65 per cent cocoa solids
4 tbsp Grand Marnier
zest of 1 orange

100g golden caster sugar
ground cinnamon, to taste
3 large eggs
icing sugar, for dusting
2 x packets of Space Dust popping candy

1.2-litre ovenproof dish, buttered

Arrange the brioche slices, overlapping, inside the dish. If the corners stick up, so much the better – everyone likes crispy bits.

Place all the remaining ingredients except the eggs, icing sugar and popping candy in a heatproof bowl set over a pan of simmering water. Once melted, remove from the heat.

In a large bowl, beat the eggs. Pour the warm chocolate mixture over the eggs and stir thoroughly.

Pour the mixture over the brioche, cover the dish, and set aside in a cool place (or the fridge) until the bread has soaked up all of the liquid. This may take up to an hour.

Preheat the oven to 200°C/gas mark 6. Cook the pudding on the top shelf for about 30 minutes. The top should be crispy while the inside is still lovely and gloopy. Remove and allow to cool for 10 minutes. Dust with icing sugar and the popping candy just before serving.

CLOVE ROCK
Northern Ireland

Although there are many clove-flavoured boiled sweets, I feel justified in placing clove rock, in particular, in Ireland. Clove rock crops up again and again from addresses in Ireland: Belfast, Kilkenny, Dublin, Enniskillen, Navan and more.

The sweet is made as a stick of rock, as explained below, red on the inside with a coating of white on the outside, but is then cut into lengths that are just the right size for sucking. It smells and tastes distinctly of cloves.

The use of cloves suggests that the sweet, like many others, would have had its origins as a medicine, designed to clear the nose and throat, and also to cleanse the palate.

Thanks to Sandra of Belfast's famous Clove Rock shop, 'Aunty Sandra's' and her nephew David Moore for this recipe. Aunty Sandra's is one of the few outlets making the rock in the old-fashioned way at the premises where it is also sold.

Practice makes perfect with sugar work. Once faced with a tray of cooling sugar you need to work fast and, as I have found, it is easier with two of you. David is a past master at this technique. Where many sweet factories might have a rock-rolling machine, at Aunty Sandra's they prefer to work by hand, as you'll see if you ever get to visit. Clove Oil is easy to find in most chemists, since it is still used to ease toothache.

250g granulated white sugar
2tbsp water
125g liquid glucose
1 tsp clove oil, or more, to taste
liquid red food colouring

icing sugar, for dusting

two 32 x 22cm baking trays, oiled
toffee scraper or wide palette knife

Heat your oven to 100°C/gas mark ¼.

Place the sugar, water and glucose in a heavy-bottomed pan, clip your sugar thermometer to the inside and bring the mixture to the boil. Continue to heat to 140°C (soft crack stage) then immediately remove the pan from the heat. Wait a few moments then divide the mixture between the trays, pouring carefully to avoid scalds. Divide the clove oil between the trays and add red food colouring to one of the trays, stirring well to combine. Place the red tray in the low oven to keep warm while you work the toffee in the other tray.

As soon as the mixture is cool enough to handle, use either a toffee scraper or wide palette knife to scoop the edges of the mixture into the

CLOVE ROCK
Northern Ireland

centre of the tray repeatedly, then work it with your hands, stretching and pulling all the time, until the mixture turns white. Repeat with the red toffee and work until it becomes opaque red.

Now, take the white batch of toffee, and roll it out with a rolling pin into a long strip about 3cm wide, oiling the toffee when necessary to keep it pliable. Take the red, and roll it into a fat sausage the same length as the white toffee. Place the red toffee on top of the white and wrap it, as though you were making a beef wellington. Trim the white toffee with a knife if you need to – it should be wrapped around in a single layer. Oil your hands then roll the toffee further, remembering to oil both it and your hands from time to time, teasing it until you have a narrow tube.

As one end of the rock gets to the correct width (slightly less than 2cm) snip off bite-sized pieces with a sharp knife or a pair of scissors. Set on a sheet of greaseproof paper, dust with icing sugar and roll the pieces in it. Leave to cool completely.

COCK ON A STICK
Nottingham

Admittedly not widely known outside of the Nottingham area and one delicacy, at least, that's unlikely to be snapped up by any multinational, the cock on a stick is part of a culinary tradition that also includes mushy peas and vinegar, all yummy treats that the citizens of Nottingham look forward to enjoying at their annual Goose Fair.

The cock on a stick is exactly as described; a cockerel-shaped sweet, generally chocolate these days, but originally made from coloured and flavoured boiled sugar. It comes in all different sizes.

The Nottingham Goose Fair, which began over 700 years ago,

COCK ON A STICK
Nottingham

was an annual autumn event that people travelled from miles around to enjoy. It gets its name from the thousands and thousands of geese driven there from all over the county. Farmers, merchants, peddlers and the like all converged on Nottingham to buy, sell, barter, gossip and carouse. The geese themselves were made to walk through something like hot pitch to toughen up their feet before the journey, which must have been something of an ordeal for the poor creatures.

But what of the cock on a stick? Definitely not as ancient as the fair itself, it's rumoured that its origins are Italian. One Ben Whitehead is said to have created the confection some time towards the end of the nineteenth century, and his forebears simply carried on. The Whitehead cocks were beautifully crafted birds that took some hours to make, and looked for all the world not like a lump of sugar but an expensive piece of Murano glass. A beautiful thing. It would be lovely to see a revival of this tradition, but I fear that the time taken in making such a lovely sweet would make it impossible to afford. The chocolate versions, though, are charming too.

This sweet doesn't come with a recipe, since as you can imagine, it's a rather elaborate confection to make at home.

COCONUT ICE

When and where coconut ice actually comes from is hard to define. The chewy coconut sweet made up of a pink layer of desiccated coconut on top of a layer of white, is often touted as a post-First World War treat but this is incorrect; I have an old recipe book with a recipe not dissimilar to the one below that's dated 1904, and coconut sweets of other types certainly existed before then. Old cookery books spell it as 'cocoa-nut', a charming version which I much prefer.

You can buy perfectly good coconut ice, generally in bars of equal parts pink and white coconut, or in bagged cubes. However, if you're fond of coconut, please have a go at making your own, because the fresh taste is far superior. In this version, I have added a little vanilla flavouring to the white part and strawberry/raspberry flavouring to the pink. You can use either condensed milk or double cream; the latter is less cloyingly sweet but the end result will need to be stored in the refrigerator.

Coconut ice has the additional benefit of needing no cooking whatsoever.

300g condensed milk or double cream
250g unsweetened desiccated coconut
300g icing sugar, plus optional extra to dust
4 drops raspberry or strawberry essence

a couple of drops of pink food colouring (or more, depending on how bright you want the shade)
4 drops vanilla essence

15cm x 20cm tin, lined with enough strong cling film to fold over the sides

Put the condensed milk and the coconut into a large bowl and sift in the icing sugar a little at a time, stirring thoroughly. As you add the sugar the mixture will get rather thick so you'll need to apply elbow grease.

Once this is done, split the mixture. To one half add the fruit essence and pink colouring; to the other add the vanilla.

Press the white mixture into the tin, followed by the pink, pressing it down neatly. Refrigerate for a couple of hours, and lift out of the tin using the cling film. Cut into squares and dust with more icing sugar if desired.

COCONUT ICE

COCONUT SWEETS or FFERINS CNAU COCO

Wales

These particular sweets, sticky, dense bars of coconut, are made to a traditional Welsh recipe which would have been made as a special treat whenever coconut was available. It's easy to forget that the ingredients we take for granted today were once considered to be rare and exotic, and recipes like this one were devised just so that everyone could have a taste. Dip the cold bars in melted chocolate and you have a delicious home-made Bounty bar!

Makes 8 bars

150ml milk
150ml water
900g golden caster sugar
30g unsalted Welsh (or other) butter, plus extra for greasing your tin

225g unsweetened desiccated coconut
1 tsp vanilla extract
red or green food colouring

20 x 20 x 2.5cm cake tin, buttered

Pour the milk and water into a heavy-bottomed pan, clip on your sugar thermometer. Bring to the boil, then tip in the caster sugar and the butter. Lower the heat, stirring all the time until the sugar and butter have melted. Bring back to the boil, cover, and boil for 2 minutes without stirring. Remove the lid and boil until your sugar thermometer reads 114.4–115.5°C (soft ball stage).

Remove from the heat immediately and stir in the coconut, tipping in a little at a time to avoid 'clumping'. Add the vanilla extract, then set the pan back on the heat, stirring until the mixture is thick and creamy.

Pour half the mixture into the buttered tin. Add the food colouring to what is left in the pan, then pour on top of the layer in the tin. Leave to cool completely, then cut it into regular pieces or bars with a sharp knife.

COLTSFOOT ROCK
Oswaldtwistle, Lancashire

When you think about it, this stuff has a pretty weird name. When I was a child I gave it a wide berth, believing that it was flavoured with the severed feet of poor little colts. I am delighted to tell you that I was wrong. Of course, what I didn't know back then was that the coltsfoot in question refers to the wild herb. The blossoms of the coltsfoot resemble dandelions, but the distinctive scalloped leaves (which appear before the flowers) resemble the hooves of the animals after whom they are named. If you prefer Latin, you can call it Tussilago farfara *Rock.*

Coltsfoot has been used for a long time – centuries, in fact – as a medicinal herb. One of its folk names (sometimes a handy hint as to a plant's properties), is coughwort. Both the juices of the plant and its distinctive leaves were used as a tonic for coughs, sore throats and even asthma. Although the use of coltsfoot was certainly not restricted to Lancashire, we can pinpoint the actual place that the rock itself originated.

In appearance, a stick of coltsfoot rock is about 15cm long; an elegantly slim, hexagonal pale beige tube. The texture of the sweet has the same delicious chalkiness as Edinburgh Rock. Sometimes you'll find the rock has been chopped into smaller, bite-sized chunks. The only people that make the traditional sticks in the UK, is Stockleys, a small but beautifully formed company based in Oswaldtwistle. Malcolm Stockley, so the story goes, was a trained sugar boiler and toffee maker, forced to take a break from his profession because of the First World War.

COLTSFOOT ROCK
Oswaldtwistle, Lancashire

Once the fighting was over, he returned to his previous trade, starting a small business in 1918 from a shed in the high street and using his kitchen at home to make the sweets. Malcolm's expertise meant that Stockleys rapidly became known for the high quality of their sweets, and the company was invited to present their confectionery at the San Francisco World Exhibition in 1939.

And the provenance of coltsfoot rock as a medicine has lasted – it's often to be found on sale at chemists and pharmacies. The original recipe called for paregoric, a tincture of opium. These days, the opium is no longer included, its inclusion in sweets now highly illegal.

CORNISH CLOTTED CREAM FUDGE
Cornwall

Whether or not fudge itself counts as a British sweet is, I confess, somewhat debatable. It might actually be an American invention. Glossing over this bombshell, however, I believe we can legitimately deck a great heap of Cornish clotted cream fudge in Union Jack bunting.

This yummy treat is exceptional, a delicious sweet that is dependent on a unique ingredient: Cornish clotted cream. (Actually, you can also get it in Devon and you can even make your own, but let's not get pedantic about that sort of thing). Clotted cream is cream that has been thickened by heating with steam and then left to cool gradually.

This fudge recipe is simple, and it is likely that you will want to make lots of it. If you'd like to adapt it, you could include nuts, chocolate chips, coconut, dried fruit … any flavourings you like. Just remember to add fruit or nuts at the end, since you don't want to cook them; chocolate chips can be added at the beating-in stage, and will melt nicely.

275g caster sugar
100g golden syrup
200ml clotted cream

1 tsp vanilla extract

20 x 20 x 5cm tray, buttered

Put all the ingredients except for the vanilla into a heavy-bottomed saucepan and clip your sugar thermometer to the inside of the pan. Heat very gently to dissolve the sugar, stirring all the while. Bring slowly to the boil, and boil for exactly 3 minutes with the lid on the pan. Remove the lid and boil, stirring, until the mixture reaches 116°C (soft ball stage). Immediately remove from the heat, add the vanilla extract and beat with a wooden spoon until the mixture is thick and creamy. Pour into the tin and leave to set for about an hour before cutting into squares with a sharp knife.

CURLY WURLY
Birmingham

When you think about it, there's not really an awful lot to many of our best sweets in terms of raw materials. Humbugs, for example? Bah. They're just boiled sugar and flavouring. The components of the Curly Wurly, a long, narrow bar made from plaited hard toffee, coated in chocolate might 'only' be chocolate and toffee, but in this case, it's the artful and ingenious arrangement of simple ingredients that makes this British sweet truly great. The Curly Wurly wouldn't be either Curly or Wurly without its characteristic shape.

David John Parfitt, an experienced confectioner working at Cadbury's in Birmingham, came up with the concept and design for the Curly Wurly in 1970 while faffing about with bits of spare toffee. However, putting the bar into factory production was tricky because of the fiddly joins in the centre of the bar. Fortunately, Birmingham's great tradition in

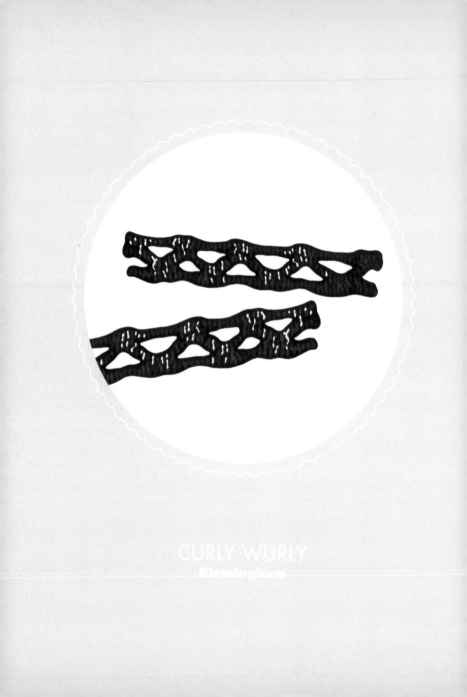

CURLY WURLY
Birmingham

industry and engineering made it the right place for this conundrum to be solved. Step up one William (Bill) Harris. It was Bill who perfected the complex piece of machinery needed to weave the toffee strands together. The early machine could weave together eight ropes of toffee, but in 1982 ambitious executives from Cadbury's commissioned a bigger, better piece of equipment, designed to boldly go where no other toffee-knitting machine had gone before ... Perfection was subsequently improved upon when a machine was built that could make not eight, not sixteen, but twenty-four ropes of glittering, golden toffee, allowing lots of bars to be made at the same time. The gloriously named Twenty-Four Rope Extruder was the brain child of Tony Wright for the Harvey Design Company.

The best way to eat a Curly Wurly, I think, is to pop it in the freezer for a couple of hours. Then, leaving the wrapper intact, rap it sharply against the edge of the kitchen table. On unwrapping the treasure you should find that a pile of chocolate shrapnel has fallen away from what is now a lattice of nude toffee, legs all crossed to preserve modesty. Naughty!

The beauty of the method I have devised here is that you can make your own version of a Curly Wurly as big as you like! It is based on a simple pulled-toffee technique since, sadly, I didn't have access to a Twenty-Four Rope Extruder.

The only tricky bit, if your predilection is for a REALLY HUGE Curly Wurly, is how to coat it in the chocolate. You will need to find a tray that is as close as possible in size to your completed toffee. The quantities given here will make two Curly Wurlies of approximately 30 x 8cm, or a single whopper of 50 x 15cm, depending on how finely you pull the toffee.

225g demerara sugar
175g golden syrup
100g unsalted butter
2 tbsp warm water
2 tsp liquid glucose
vanilla flavouring (optional)
400g chocolate (plain, milk or
  white)

baking tray large enough to
  accommodate your chosen size
  of Curly Wurly, buttered
scraping tool

Put all the ingredients for the toffee, apart from the flavouring, into a heavy-bottomed pan, attaching your sugar thermometer to the inside. Over a low heat, stir the contents until the sugar has dissolved.

Bring to the boil, without stirring and heat to 130°C (hard ball stage). Immediately remove the pan from the heat. Pour the toffee carefully into the tray and leave to cool for a few moments.

When the toffee has started to set at the edges of the tray, take your scraping tool and scoop the edges of the toffee into the centre. Repeat until cool enough to handle, then begin to pull and twist the ball of toffee into a long rope of about 5mm thick. As you do so, it will become paler in colour and creamy in texture. With practice, making ropes of regular thickness will become easier.

Divide the toffee into three roughly equal strands. (If you have a manu-factured Curly Wurly to hand, copy it). Use one strand to form a rectan-gular 'frame', sticking it together in one corner. Then, starting in the top left-hand corner, zigzag the second strand down and across the frame all along its length, finishing in the bottom right-hand corner. Repeat the design the other way up with the third strand of toffee, starting from the top right-hand corner. Where the toffee overlaps, press it down to seal it. If, during the construction process, the toffee has started to set and the pieces refuse to glue together, heat the tip of a knife in hot water and use it to soften the junctions; they will stick down nicely. Set aside in a cool place for 15 minutes or so, until the toffee is completely firm.

Melt the chocolate in a bain marie and then, depending on the size of your toffee lattice(s), either dip it in the chocolate, brush it on, or coat it on with a spoon. Leave the chocolate coating to set before you turn the Curly Wurly over to coat the underside.

DEVON DOUBLE CREAM CARAMELS
Devon

In these caramels (a soft toffee), the star of the show is the thick Devon cream that gives the sweet the most superb flavour and texture. And it's because of the lush pastures of the county that the cream is so lovely. Yes, we might complain about the rain sometimes in the UK, but this sweet is proof that the iffy weather has a distinct upside. Epitomising the admirably stoic British trait of making the most of a bad lot when it comes to the weather, this irresistible treat has quite rightly earned its place as a truly great British sweet.

360ml Devon double cream
200g granulated sugar
210g soft light brown sugar
2 tsp salt
2 tsp vanilla extract

20 x 20 x 5cm baking tray, buttered
wet pastry brush

Put all the ingredients except for the vanilla into a heavy-bottomed saucepan and clip your sugar thermometer to the inside of the pan. Over a low heat, stir the ingredients until the sugars have dissolved, then turn up the heat, stirring all the time so that the cream doesn't burn. Bring to the boil, using the wet pastry brush to push down any sugar granules that might accumulate on the sides of the pan. Boil until your sugar thermometer reads 118°C (hard ball stage), then immediately remove from the heat. Wait a few moments then stir in the vanilla extract. Pour the mixture into the tray and when the caramel is set, cut into squares (mine were about 4cm). If you like, you could dip the cooled caramels in melted chocolate.

EDINBURGH ROCK
Edinburgh, Scotland

Sweets that are named after places are more common in Scotland and the Borders than in any other part of the UK. Quite why this is I have yet to fathom, but one of the best-known of these Caledonian sweets is Edinburgh Rock. This delicate confection – short tubes of powdery textured, pastel-coloured sweets – whose availability is certainly not restricted to the nation's capital, is yet another sweet legendarily believed to have come into the world because of a mistake.

Alexander Ferguson was born in Doune, in Perthshire, central Scotland, in 1798. In later years he would be known by the name of 'Sweetie Sandy'. Keen on messing about with sugar from an early age, Sandy's childhood hobby of playing with boiling sugar and various flavourings was looked at askance by his father, who preferred that his son took up his own rather more butch profession as a joiner. Sandy persisted with his passion, though, and eventually moved to Glasgow to learn the art and craft of the confectioner. After his training, Sandy moved to Edinburgh, and it was here that the reputed 'happy accident' took place. The story goes that having made a batch of 'normal' rock (see page 84), the hard candy was accidentally left out for some time (possibly weeks, but sadly this is not recorded) and went soft, resulting in the

EDINBURGH ROCK
Edinburgh, Scotland

distinctively delicious chalky texture of Edinburgh rock. Good job that Sandy didn't throw it away. Whether the story is true or just an inventive bit of PR is not confirmed, but a look at the ingredients for both 'normal' rock and Edinburgh rock might give us a clue.

'Normal' rock is made from a mixture of sugar, glucose syrup, and flavourings, traditionally peppermint. Modern recipes for Edinburgh rock, on the other hand, additionally list cream of tartar. For the purposes of boiling sugar, this ingredient is generally added to prevent heated sugar from crystallising. We don't know whether Sandy would have added it – it may be that leaving it out was enough to soften the basic rock recipe – but it certainly is a fundamental part of commercial versions today.

Sandy returned to Doune and bought himself a nice big house. In 1893, some eighteen years after his death, the street in which he had been born was named 'Sweetie Lane' in his honour.

450g granulated sugar
200ml water
pinch of cream of tartar
colourings and flavourings of your choice, matching or otherwise – peppermint, rose or how about lavender (my friend Theo insists on fiery ginger Edinburgh rock; I am beginning to think he's addicted)

icing sugar, for dusting
a willing friend (see Theo, above)

separate baking tray for each flavour, large enough to use as a work surface (38cm x 30cm is good), buttered

Preheat the oven to 100°C/gas mark ¼.

Before you start, decide how many different flavour/colour combinations you are going to make, and butter the according number of baking trays. Don't make too many different choices if this is your first time making Edinburgh rock as you will need to handle the contents of each tray, which gets trickier as the mixture cools. If you have a friend on hand it will be easier.

Tip the sugar and water into a heavy-bottomed saucepan and clip on your sugar thermometer. Heat the mixture over a low heat, stirring all the while until the sugar has dissolved completely. Bring to the boil, then boil steadily until the mixture reaches 129°C (hard ball stage). Immediately take the pan off the heat and stir in the cream of tartar, making sure there are no lumps. Allow the mixture to cool for a few minutes.

Divide the mixture equally between the trays and stir in the colouring and flavourings. A couple of drops of each should be enough as Edinburgh rock is traditionally pastel-coloured. Using a scraper or a palette knife, keep folding the sides of the mixture into the middle. This is where your friend will come in handy, but if one of the trays cools down too much, just place it in a low oven until it becomes pliable once more. As soon as the mix is cool enough to handle, sift icing sugar over your work surface and dust your hands. Knead the sugar until it loses its gloss and becomes matte. Pull carefully into long, neat sticks; about 12cm is a good length.

Sandy had success with Edinburgh rock because he forgot all about it. You have to do the same thing with yours. Cut into 12cm sticks, then cut one stick into smaller pieces (for testing the consistency), and set the Edinburgh rock aside at room temperature for 24 hours. After this time, one of the test pieces should taste slightly powdery and soft. If not, leave longer. When the sticks are at the desired consistency, wrap the bundle in greaseproof paper and store in an airtight container.

EVERTON TOFFEE
Everton, Liverpool

The Everton district of Liverpool is famous for at least two things: the lovely buttery toffees which you can eat, and 'the Toffees', the Everton football team, which is nicknamed after them.

Everton toffee is featured in a lovely old etched advertisement, which claims that the original Everton toffee was established in 1753. The advertisement reads:

THE WORLD-FAMED ORIGINAL EVERTON TOFFEE

Established 1753
As Supplied to
Her Majesty the Queen
His Royal Highness the Duke of Cambridge
Lord John Russell
and Manufactured only by
R.H.Wignall
Late of the Original Toffee Shop
Who is Grandson to
Molly Bushell
the Original Inventor and the only Person in the World in Possession
of the Original Family Recipe, of Which Not Even a Single Copy Has
Been Taken, Consequently All Others are only Imitations.

Popular history also tells us that it was one Molly Bushell, nee Johnson, who invented the toffee. Apparently she was given the recipe by an anonymous physician, who, we must presume, prescribed it as a tonic. Molly, who plied her sticky wares in the mid-eighteenth century, wasn't the only confectioner in Everton. In 1894 the company that she had started was sold to a rival, Nobletts, who used a stylised drawing of

EVERTON TOFFEE
Everton, Liverpool

Molly on their label which gave rise to a rumour that it was this fictional character who was the real purveyor of the toffees.

Everton toffee has a rich, buttery taste, and luckily the recipe, once so jealously guarded, is now readily available.

100g unsalted butter
225g granulated or demerara
  sugar
225g golden syrup

20 x 20cm baking tin, buttered
toffee hammer

Melt the butter in a heavy-bottomed pan, clipping your sugar thermometer to the inside, then add the sugar and syrup, stirring all the while until everything has dissolved. Bring up to 143°C (hard crack stage) then simply pour the molten mixture into the tray and leave to set for 15 minutes or so. Smash up with a toffee hammer.

Store Everton toffee wrapped in greaseproof paper in an airtight container in a cool place where it will stay fresh for a week. Left out, it will become very sticky indeed.

FISHERMAN'S FRIEND
Fleetwood, Lancs

Fleetwood is a fishing port in Lancashire on the west coast of England, often cold and lashed with freezing gales. It was here that the tongue-tingling Fisherman's Friend – beige-coloured sucky sweets with a powerful flavour of aniseed – were invented in 1865.

James Lofthouse, a young pharmacist, noticed that his local fishermen were in dire need of something to alleviate the irritation of their severest sniffles. He concocted a devastatingly strong tincture, made

FISHERMAN'S FRIEND
Fleetwood, Lancs

from eucalyptus and menthol, that would cut through the snottiest of symptoms. However, the medicine was contained in bottles, which were, of course, prone to breakages on board the trawlers. To resolve this problem James had the brainwave of transforming the liquid into a flat lozenge, which could be carried by the frostbitten fishermen. So grateful were those seafarers, that they nicknamed the little lozenges 'friends'. Whether James Lofthouse had called them anything else prior to this, we don't know. What we do know is that the sweets worked so well that today, the fifth generation of the Lofthouse dynasty still runs the factory in Fleetwood. Employing some 300 people, they're the biggest employer in the town.

It is clear that, among the old-established sweet companies, the ones that do best are those that have a star product that doesn't need an awful lot of embellishment, and whose owners and managers have avoided the temptation to diversify too much. Fisherman's Friend follows this pattern precisely. I spoke to Martin Stimson, who works for Impex, who are devoted to the sale of Fisherman's Friend all over the world. Martin told me that when James Lofthouse invented the lozenges they were immediately popular, and sold from two shops, but that nothing much happened for the next hundred years. Then, in the 1960s, a lady called Doreen married Tony Lofthouse, the great-great-grandson of James. Doreen reckoned that the tourists flocking to the town in the summer might like to buy Fisherman's Friend lozenges to take home with them as a souvenir. And she was right. In 1974 a meeting between Doreen and the founder of Impex, Ivan Gibson, led to the export of a colossal 96 per cent of what the factory in Fleetwood was making. Today 4.5 billion of those powdery little lozenges are sold around the world every year and a quarter of these sales are in the Far East, where the sweets aren't viewed as medicinal at all. Flavours include spicy mandarin, cherry and blackcurrant.

It's testament to James Lofthouse's ingenuity that, despite the addition of flavourings for the Far East market, the recipe has remained virtually unchanged since the day he invented it. A concoction of menthol, eucalyptus, sugar or sorbitol, liquorice and aniseed is all it takes. Although, I am warned, to try to make a Fisherman's Friend at home wouldn't be worth the effort. It's much easier to nip down to the chemist and buy them.

FRUIT PASTILLES
York

A 'pastille', in French, is a small lozenge, often scented. Although fruit pastes had been made in Britain for years (quince was particularly popular) we didn't have access to the vital ingredient gum tragacanth – or gum dragon, as it was known – until it was introduced to the Rowntree factory in the late 1870s by an itinerant French gum salesman. This is how, in 1881, Rowntree subsequently broke the French monopoly on pastille-type sweets.

Rowntree began in York. Mary Tuke, a Quaker, opened a small grocery in the town in 1725. When she died, her nephew William inherited the business and invested heavily in an exciting new ingredient – cocoa. In 1860 another Quaker, Henry Rowntree, joined the business, joined later by his brother Joseph.

At the time, Quakers in Britain (and, indeed, in other parts of Europe) were persecuted because of their beliefs and certain paths were closed to them. Quakers were not even permitted to go to University. The strict moral code of the Quakers explains why so many British confectionery companies have Quaker origins; chocolate was seen as a wholesome alternative to the evils of drink. Their ethical values also explain why these same Quaker companies offered such good conditions for their workers, too: holidays, pension schemes, equal rights for women, even model villages (Cadbury built Bourneville, for example, and Rowntree built New Earswick) to house their workers.

The secret of making a perfect Rowntree's-style Fruit Pastille is closely guarded and it would be pointless to try to emulate them at home. However, here's a delicious recipe for a Fruit Pastille type of sweet, using oodles of real fruit. It's a great way to use up a glut of a particular crop, but be sure to use fruit that will reduce down to a pulpy gloop such as apples, pears, plums or quince, or you can supplement the same quantity of softer fruits (berries, peeled peaches, nectarines, plums and mango) with up to 30 per cent of pulped apples to give the same effect. You could even use carrots in the mix although they need to be cooked a little longer.

900g fruit, peeled and cored
caster sugar (for weight, see recipe
   below), plus extra for coating
juice of 1 lemon

20 x 20 x 5cm baking tray, lined
   with non-stick baking paper

Place the fruit in a wide heavy-bottomed pan (or a jam pan if you have one), with just enough water to cover. Bring to the boil, making sure that the fruit doesn't 'catch' on the bottom of the pan. Simmer over a low heat for about an hour until the fruit is soft, then allow to cool a little before passing through a sieve into a bowl. Weigh the resulting purée.

Return the purée to the pan with its equivalent weight of sugar and the lemon juice. Over a low heat, stir until the sugar has completely dissolved then bring to the boil. Boil rapidly, stirring, until the mixture starts to thicken.

Reduce the heat and continue to simmer for 5 minutes, then test for setting point using the saucer test. Put a saucer or plate in the freezer for 15 minutes. Take a small amount of purée in a teaspoon and place on the cold saucer for a few seconds. If the surface wrinkles when you push it with your finger, the mixture is set.

FRUIT PASTILLES
York

At this point, pour the thick, syrupy mixture into the prepared tray and leave aside overnight to set completely. Once set, cut into cubes, then roll in the caster sugar, coating thoroughly.

GOBSTOPPERS

If sweets, like plants, were divided into species, then the gobstopper would belong to the genus 'comfit', a word which itself is derived from confectionery. A comfit is comprised of a central core – originally, perhaps, a nut – covered in a sugar coating. The sophisticated and elegant sugared almond (see page 148) may be the posh elderly aunt of the oafish gobstopper, but they belong to the same family.

In the USA gobstoppers are known as 'jawbreakers', with very good reason. They're excruciatingly hard, and sometimes too big to get into your mouth. If you were to attempt to bite down on one this could be injurious to your pride as well as to your teeth. For some years I had a very large gobstopper, some 6–8cm across. I kept it in captivity, in a jar, all on its own. Grown-ups could never guess what it actually was; children, of course, with an instinct for sugar and more given to experimentation, knew its exact nature. Sadly, after some years, my giant gobstopper met its match in the form of a visiting old English bulldog who rolled it about with his nose and then slobbered over it for a while before he carried it away and hid it. The gobstopper has never been seen again. No doubt it's still gathering dust and fluff under a sofa somewhere.

The gobstopper constitutes a satisfyingly sound pocket money investment for children, since they last such a long time. Some gobstoppers can last for days, if not weeks. What happens between sucks is a somewhat shady area, a private matter between the gobstopper and its owner.

GOBSTOPPERS

The first mention we have of a gobstopper is a literary one. In 1928 Walter de la Mare, in his anthological work Come Hither, writes: 'Gobstoppers and toffee ... are these not good names for goodies?'. However, it's a later literary invention that is credited with making the gobstopper world famous. Willie Wonka, owner of the famous Chocolate Factory, invents the ultimate sweet, the 'everlasting gobstopper'. This kind of gobstopper never gets smaller, no matter how long you suck it. The magical sweet leapt from Roald Dahl's page and into real life in 1976 after a company called Breaker Confections in Chicago licensed the rights to use the Willie Wonka name. Nestlé now own the brand.

We know that gobstoppers have existed for at least one hundred years, but the name of the genius who invented them is sadly lost to us. We can only wonder at how he or she stumbled on the process. A commercial gobstopper takes a while to make. A central core – perhaps one grain of sugar or the seed of a star anise – is coated with many layers of different-coloured sugar. The sweets are made in large pans which rotate and tumble the gobstopper at the same time, coating it in successive layers of differently coloured sugar. It's a time-consuming process. Speaking of which, it is also possible to make your own gobstoppers at home, but having tried it, I would say don't bother; it'll drive you round the bend.

HAWICK BALLS
Hawick

Aaah, Hawick. Home not only to some of the finest cashmere and woollen manufacturers in the world (including, no less, the very posh Pringle company), but also to the renowned Hawick Balls. These lovely buttery, minty little globes of joy look a bit like a pickled onion, but the recipe is a 'closely guarded secret' known only to the makers, the Golden Casket people of Greenock where the balls are now created. I'm guessing that the real secret is in the blend of mint oils that are used in the sweets – I could, of course, be wrong.

Hawick Balls were first made, apparently, by a lady called Jessie McVitie in the 1850s. She followed the ingenious method, fashionable at the time, of pulling her boiled toffee mixture by hanging it on a hook and allowing gravity to do the rest.

Hawick Balls are inextricably linked to the late, great, Bill McLaren, a Hawick boy who grew up to become a national treasure. Bill was a renowned rugby commentator, whose love of these mints propelled them to (almost) stratospheric heights of fame. People loved Bill for his witty ad libs about the antics on the pitch: 'He's like a demented ferret up a wee drainpipe', for example, or, 'He kicked that ball like it was three pounds of haggis.' Or then there's, 'My goodness, that wee ball's gone so high there'll be snow on it when it comes down.' The quote that's most apt to this story, however, is, 'Would you like a Hawick Ball, son?' Famously, Bill carried a 'poke' of mints about his person at all times and was ever-generous with them … Except, apparently, to members of the England rugby team, whom he always managed to overlook.

If you would like to try making Hawick Balls, you need to lower yourself to bribery and corruption to try to wring the secret out of their makers. I have tried, and failed.

HUMBUGS
Somewhere in the North. Probably.

Although the tradition of striped, pulled sugar sweets and their technique were known, and used, in medieval Arabia, the first humbugs appeared on British shores in the middle of the nineteenth century.

And while I say humbugs are 'probably' from the north of England, this is based purely on my reading of Elizabeth Gaskell's Sylvia's Lovers, published in 1863: 'He had provided himself with a paper of humbugs for the child – "humbugs" being the North-country term for certain lumps of toffy, well-flavoured with peppermint.'

As to the origins and etymology of the glorious word 'humbug' itself, there is some debate, although we do know from the Shorter Oxford Dictionary that it first came into common use between 1730 and 1769. The most common definition is that a humbug is a 'hoax' or a 'trick' and was derived from an Italian phrase, 'Uomo Bugiardo', which means, literally, 'lying man'. (The Wizard of Oz describes himself as 'just a humbug' and, of course, Charles Dickens' Ebeneezer Scrooge mutters 'Bah! Humbug!' in relation to Christmastime). As well as the more common humbug – the stripy lump of solid sugar with a mint flavour – I also discovered a humbug indigenous to Taunton, which startles the happy sucker when he or she reaches the centre of the sweet. The middle isn't sugar at all, but an almond. Perhaps this is the true 'humbug', a trick played on the customer? Whatever the case, we do know that mint oils and extracts, as well as those of clove and wintergreen, were used as cold cures in the dark days before cane sugar landed on our shores. The addition of sugar was a very welcome way of making almost any medicine palatable. Humbugs are an absolute joy to make and a good way to practise your sugar-pulling and twisting techniques.

450g demerara sugar
150ml water
50g butter
a pinch of cream of tartar
flavouring (mint is traditional)
black food colouring (powdered)

icing sugar, for dusting your hands

two 38 x 30cm shallow baking
  trays, oiled
scissors, the blades dipped in oil

Place all the ingredients, except for the flavouring and colour, in a heavy-bottomed pan and attach your sugar thermometer. Put the pan

HUMBUGS
Somewhere in the North. Probably.

JELLY BABIES
Yorkshire and Lancashire

over a low heat until the sugar has all dissolved. Bring slowly to the boil and boil steadily to 143°C (soft crack stage) then remove from the heat immediately. Leave to cool for a few minutes, then pour half the mixture on to one of the tins and add the colouring and flavouring to the remaining mixture in the pan. Stir well and pour into the second tray.

When the mixture can be handled comfortably, find a friend to help you. Both of you should dust your hands with icing sugar before you each start to manipulate a tray of toffee, folding and pulling it into long strips approximately 3cm thick. This should take no more than 10 minutes. If you don't have a friend, leave one tray in a warm oven until you're ready to give it the same treatment. Twist the two different-coloured strips together; they will stick to one another. Then pull the entire strip of toffee until it's about 2cm wide, and snip into bite-sized lengths with the oiled scissors. Roll in icing sugar. (The humbugs. Not you.)

JELLY BABIES
Yorkshire and Lancashire

How do you eat your jelly baby? This is a crucial test of your personality. Kindly and humane sweet enthusiasts bite the heads off first and put the poor things out of their misery. Starting to eat your jelly babies at the feet, on the other hand, is a sure sign of a cruel streak. If you start from the sides, you're a confused combination of the two.

The preferred sweet of several incarnations of Doctor Who (the character, not the actors), the jelly baby has a curious history. In 1864, Steinboch, an Austrian confectioner at the Fryer's sweet makers in Lancashire, came up with the idea for a sweet shaped like a baby, which went on sale by the name of 'unclaimed babies'. Alas, the new sweet didn't take off and Steinboch's 'babies' remained, for the most part, unclaimed. However, in 1918 the Bassett Company of Sheffield launched the more familiar jelly babies that many of us know and love. They were called 'peace babies' in celebration of the end of the First World War. Rationing during the Second World War meant that production of the peace babies was put on hold, but in 1953 the sweets arrived on the shelves again, renamed as jelly babies, and they have been going strong ever since. Schoolchildren that are lucky enough to have particularly imaginative science teachers have experienced the 'screaming jelly baby' phenomenon, in which potassium chlorate powder is melted in a test tube using heat from a Bunsen burner. A jelly baby sacrifice placed in the test tube bursts into flame while emitting a loud screaming sound. Fabulously cruel but fascinatingly incendiary!

For obvious reasons of moulding/shaping, it would be impossible to try and re-create jelly babies yourself, but have a go at this sweet-based ice cream. It's such an easy recipe, which doesn't require either an ice-cream maker or the freeze and frequent stir routine.

Jelly Baby Ice Cream

Serves 4–6

200g condensed milk
600ml double cream

1 tsp vanilla extract
20 jelly babies

Put all the ingredients except for the jelly babies into a large bowl, then beat either by hand or with an electric whisk, until you have a thick, creamy mixture. Gently stir in the jelly babies. Freeze the mixture for a couple of hours or until solid, removing from the freezer 15 minutes before serving. An easy and fun dessert for parties!

KENDAL MINT CAKE
Kendal, Cumbria

Play word association with the word 'Kendal', and 'mint cake' is offered up every single time. It's uncanny. I know, because I tried it recently.

What is probably not so well known, however, is that the thirteenth Dalai Lama was a big fan of the stuff. It was presented to him by Dr Theodore Howard Somervell, who took part in the 1922 and 1924 British Mount Everest expeditions. Since then, Kendal Mint Cake – the slim, white or brown minty bar – has become the benchmark sweet for mountaineers and explorers and is the stuff of minty legend. Even walkers intending to pace to the local pub and back know that mint cake will do the job of providing sustenance should disaster strike.

As with so many of our great British sweets, rumour has it that Kendal Mint Cake was created by accident. In 1869, intending to make a clear, glacier-type mint, Joseph Wiper, a young confectioner living in Kendal, took his eye off the pan of boiling sugar for a moment and the sugar started to granulate, resulting in a mixture that was opaque and grainy rather than translucent and smooth. Left to cool, the result was the awe-inspiring mint cake, which put the small town of Kendal on the map. Wiper's name remained on the wrappers of the mint cake for 107 years. In 1987 the last descendent of Joseph Wiper retired and the firm of Romney's proudly took over the Kendal Mint Cake manufacturing.

You may find some recipes for Kendal Mint Cake include milk, but the genuine article is made with water. (With thanks to John Barron of Romney's for this recipe.)

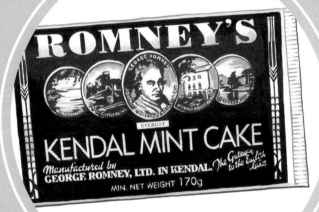

KENDAL MINT CAKE
Kendal, Cumbria

Makes two 100g bars

250g granulated sugar
250g glucose
25–30ml water

¼ tsp strongly flavoured peppermint oil, or to taste

20cm x 20cm baking tray, oiled

Put the sugar, water and glucose into a small heavy-bottomed pan. Attach your sugar thermometer to the inside of the pan. Bring to the boil, then continue to heat to 115°C (soft ball stage) and immediately remove from the heat.

Allow to cool, stirring constantly, brushing down any granulating sugar from the sides of the pan – this will take up to 20 minutes. Add the peppermint oil. Stir for 10 minutes, until the mixture is starting to turn creamy coloured and opaque, then carefully pour the liquid into the tin and leave to set. Mark into two bars, or break into shards. If stored in greaseproof paper in an airtight tin, Kendal Mint Cake will last indefinitely.

LEMON DROPS
(or lime, or orange, or cherry)

The lemon drop, a bright yellow round sweet with a powdery coating, shot to prominence for many people after it was revealed to be the favoured sweet of Professor Dumbledore, a much-loved character in the Harry Potter stories by J.K. Rowling. It is simply a timeless favourite, found in all traditional sweet shops, whose provenance is unknown but which is thought to date back to at least the mid nineteenth century.

120g white caster sugar
100ml water
½ tsp cream of tartar
2 tsp citric acid
½ tsp lemon extract

6 drops yellow food colouring
icing sugar, sifted, for rolling and
    dusting the shaped sweets

20 x 30cm baking tray, lightly oiled

Preheat the oven to 100°C/gas mark ¼.

Put the sugar, cream of tartar and water into a heavy-bottomed pan, clip a sugar thermometer to the inside of the pan and cook over a low heat until the sugar has dissolved. Continue to heat until the mixture reaches 143°C (soft crack stage), then remove from the heat and pour into the baking tray. Allow to cool for 2–3 minutes then sprinkle over the citric acid, lemon extract and the colouring. Use a scraper to scoop the edges of the toffee into the centre repeatedly to mix in the added ingredients. When cool enough to handle, take some of the toffee and roll into a strip about a centimetre wide and snip into 2.5cm pieces with a pair of oiled scissors. Keep the remaining toffee in a baking tray in a warm oven to keep it pliable as you work. The individual sweets can be shaped into balls after snipping with the scissors. Sprinkle the sweets with icing sugar once they are shaped.

NB To make different-flavoured drops but with that same satisfyingly sour flavour, substitute the lemon extract for the flavour you prefer.

LIQUORICE
Pontefract, Yorkshire

Liquorice comes from a plant that has a real spell-check befuddler of a name; Glycyrrhiza glabra. *The first part of this name originates in a*

LIQUORICE
Pontefract, Yorkshire

Greek word meaning 'sweet root' and the second part, 'glabra', means 'hairless' or 'smooth'. The plant itself is small, scruffy and undignified-looking. It is not indigenous to the British Isles; rather it grows in the wild in the Middle East and Asia, and has been used – and is still used – as a medicine long before it became a sweet confection

According to legend, the plant was introduced to Yorkshire by the Dominican monks who arrived in Pontefract in the eleventh century; the monks were known for their cultivation of medicinal herbs so this is not an unlikely theory. It's unlikely that we will ever know the truth, but what we do know is that the liquorice plant flourished in Yorkshire's soft, deep, fertile soil, despite the rain and occasional harsh climate.

The sweet that put Pontefract on the map is my mum's favourite – the Pontefract cake. These small round discs of sweetened liquorice – sometimes called Yorkshire pennies – were first 'invented' by Sir George Saville about a hundred years before a different little George tampered with the recipe and changed the course of history. Although accounts of the story have become a bit fuzzy, the consensus is that around 1760 the young George Dunhill, who in later years would become a chemist, is credited with the master stroke that transformed liquorice from tonic to treat. Given a cake as medicine and, as we might guess, hating the taste, the young George made his own version, tampering with the recipe and adding sugar, presumably to make it more palatable. Thus, in the hands of callow youth do empires quake.

In the early 1900s there were 10 factories manufacturing the pennies in and around Pontefract. The resulting Pontefract cakes were then stamped by hand with the distinctive seal, a method which lasted right up until the early 1960s. During times in which there was no such thing as RSI, the experienced 'thumper' could stamp out up to 30,000 of the Yorkshire pennies every day.

In fact, the seal used for the Pontefract cakes had a part to play in an aspect of life which some might consider – mistakenly – to be more important than mere confections: politics. We take secret ballots for granted now, but prior to 1872 they didn't exist at all. In that year, the first secret ballot, in which an anonymous X was placed next to the name of the preferred candidate, took place in Pontefract. This was a major step forward for the democratic process; prior to 1872 votes were declared publicly which meant that bribery and corruption were rife. After the voting was completed the ballot box was made tamper-proof by means of a wax seal; and in the groundbreaking ballot of 1872, the stamp from the Pontefract cakes was used to set the wax seal on the box. Whether this was because of pride in the Yorkshire pennies or whether it was a signal of disdain for the whole new system is a matter for conjecture.

Today, liquorice comes in myriad shapes and styles, colours and flavours. Bootlaces, pipes, sticks, hollow tubes full of kali (like sherbet, except with a larger grain), liquorice allsorts (see below) … What's your favourite? This recipe will give you the scope to make lots of different shapes.

200g molasses
1 tsp ground liquorice root
1 tsp ground star anise
150g plain flour

2 drops black food colouring
½ tsp salt
icing sugar, for dusting

Place the molasses in a pan over a low heat, then add the ground liquorice and star anise.

Sift the flour and add it to the molasses a little at a time until you have a soft but workable dough. You might need a little more or a little less flour. Leave the 'dough' in a cool place for 30 minutes to set.

You can then make any shapes you like. Roll into tubes, or if you cut into rounds about 2.5cm in diameter, you have your own Pontefract cakes which you can then personalise with your own 'seal'. Dust your shapes with icing sugar to finish.

This liquorice will harden in time even when stored wrapped in grease-proof paper in an airtight container. If this happens, warm in a low oven for a couple of minutes.

LIQUORICE ALLSORTS
Sheffield

This lovely jumble of liquorice-laden lovelies came about when in 1899 a gentleman called Charlie Thompson, a salesman for the Bassett Company, dropped a box of samples of liquorice sweets during a meeting with a buyer in Leicester. The buyer apparently pointed out how attractive the mixture was and quickly placed an order for the motley collection. Bassett's liquorice allsorts soon went into mass production. Open a bag of allsorts today and you will generally pick out one of ten different types of sweet, among them 'the coconut one', the 'jelly one' (aniseed-flavoured jelly covered in tiny sugar dots) or a variety of other sweets made from liquorice and fondant layered into cubes or discs.

Bertie Bassett, the cheery chap who is constructed from liquorice allsorts, made his first appearance as the Bassett mascot in 1929 and today even appears in a cameo role in the packet. He's a small black liquorice sweet and is something of a prize to find in your bag. Bertie is actually married to Betty; their wedding took place in Sheffield in 2009. Some rude people have accused this of being a sham marriage, a stunt designed to attract the attention of the paparazzi and boost sales of the sweets. What nonsense.

LIQUORICE ALLSORTS
Sheffield

LOSHIN DU
South Wales

Loshin Du means 'black sweets' so it's reasonable to suppose that the recipe that follows here could well be for the 'black sweets' referred to in the well-known Welsh poem, 'The Lady of Kidwelly'. The poem tells the story of the Lady Hawise de Londres, (the rightful heiress to the Norman Kidwelly Castle) who had to disguise herself as a humble peddler of sweets to gain access to her home after it was captured by the Welsh in the thirteenth century.

There are several recipes from Wales for what is essentially a basic treacle toffee but in this case it I have used the one with the minimum of ingredients, my reasoning being that anyone making such in the nineteenth century (or earlier) in Wales would have made it as simply as possible, hence there are far fewer ingredients in this recipe than for, say Bonfire Toffee (see page 56) or its north Welsh counterpart, taffi triog (see page 153). There are no fancy gadgets used either; this toffee would have been made on a range or maybe even an open fire and there would certainly have not been anything as fancy as a sugar thermometer.

225g black treacle
225g demerara sugar
1 tbsp Welsh (or other) butter

32cm x 22cm shallow baking tray, buttered
toffee hammer (optional)

Place all the ingredients in a heavy-bottomed pan and clip your thermometer to the inside of the pan. Heat gently, stirring until everything has dissolved, then continue to heat, stirring all the while, until you reach 152°C (hard crack stage). Immediately remove the pan from the heat and pour the mixture carefully into the tray.

If you prefer a regularly shaped toffee, score it into squares after 5–10 minutes then leave to set (this will take about 30 minutes depending on the ambient temperature), otherwise shatter with a toffee hammer when hard.

LOVE HEARTS
Derbyshire

To fully appreciate the small, fizzy, message-bearing sweet that is the Love Heart, we have to look to its ancestors, namely, the conversation and motto lozenges of yesteryear. Conversation lozenges were popular during the rather repressed Victorian era, and the slogans written on them speak of a shy, tongue-tied generation who flirted via sweets: 'Can You Polka?' and 'How Do You Flirt?' were amongst the messages on the sweets made by the Terry's company in York. (The ones made by Thomas Handisyde in London had to be sucked to make the message appear.) In a similar vein, the motto lozenges used by the Temperance Society to convey their manifesto must have been huge. Instructions included snappy slogans as 'Sobriety is the sure way to riches' and 'Hard work does not need intoxicating liquor'.

Brothers Alfred and Maurice Matlow started selling jelly sweets on a stall in East London in the 1920s. In 1928 they created a factory and in 1933 they merged with Swizzels, a rival sweet-maker specialising in fizzy sweets to share factory space. In 1954, inspiration struck and Love Hearts were born, initially as a 'prize' inside a Christmas cracker, with the words 'I Love You' inscribed into the sugar tablet, before other messages were added.

As times and fashions have changed, the messages on Love Hearts have also altered. For instance, for a glorious period in the 1950s you could suck on a Love Heart that read 'Hey Daddio' or 'Far Out, Man'.

These were phased out before the end of the 1950s, though, and by the end of the 1960s you couldn't find a Love Heart with 'Cool' written on it either, presumably because by then it was deemed uncool! Today any one of 134 different missives could greet you from the colourful paper tube. Occasionally a message has proved problematic, such as the encouraging 'Drop Dead Gorgeous' which, too long to fit on the sweet, was accidentally shortened to 'Drop Dead', and thus discontinued. 'Email Me', introduced in 1998, is still going strong but at the time of writing hasn't been joined by 'Tweet Me'. It's only a matter of time.

Trying to emulate Love Hearts at home is an impossible task, but Swizzels Matlow themselves gave me the following recipe. It's a girlie little snack which boys will wolf down, so hold them back at the kitchen door.

Mini Love Hearts Cupcakes

50g unsalted butter, at room
   temperature
50g golden caster sugar
50g self-raising flour
¼ tsp baking powder
1 large egg, beaten
1 tsp vanilla extract

FOR THE TOPPING
75g unsalted butter, at room
   temperature
175g icing sugar, sifted
1 tsp strawberry flavouring
1 packet of Mini Love Hearts

a 36-hole mini muffin tin
36 mini muffin cases

Preheat the oven to 170°C/gas mark 3½.

For the cupcakes, cream the butter with the sugar in a blender or with the back of a wooden spoon. Sift together the flour and baking powder and fold into the mixture. Gradually fold in the egg and the vanilla extract to form a smooth and creamy batter.

LOVE HEARTS

Derbyshire

Divide the batter evenly between the paper cases and place in the oven for about 10 minutes (because the cakes are small, they don't take long to bake). Remove from the oven and leave to cool completely in the tin.

For the topping, cream the butter, add the sifted icing sugar and mix in well with the occasional drop or two of water. Add the flavouring and beat until you have a smooth paste.

Put the mix into a piping bag and pipe a swirl on to each cupcake, placing a Mini Love Heart on each. Wait 15 minutes for the icing to set, then arrange on a pretty plate.

MACAROON BARS
Scotland and Ireland

In Scotland and Ireland, macaroon bars were traditionally made with potatoes. Whenever there were any mashed spuds left over from dinner, they were magically transformed into the chewy coconut bars, flavoured with vanilla and sometimes coated in chocolate. There's a lot to be said for a 'waste not, want not' philosophy and though the thought of potato in a sweet might seem alien, bear in mind that both sweet potatoes and potatoes were once considered not only a delicacy but an aphrodisiac, just like sugar.

You can buy commercial versions of the macaroon bar, though they are not often found outside of Scotland or Ireland. The shop-bought article dispenses with the spud because of issues of shelf life, and instead is made from a simple fondant of sugar and egg. It's well worth having a go at making the traditional version though – once you get over the novelty of putting potatoes into sweets, they're quite delicious. Ask your friends what they think the main ingredient is.

MACAROON BARS

Scotland and Ireland

Makes 8 bars

1 large, floury potato (such as
 Desiree, King Edward or Maris
 Piper), peeled and cut into
 medium, regular chunks
500g icing sugar
250g bar of good-quality chocolate
 (plain or milk)

200g unsweetened desiccated
 coconut
a couple of drops of vanilla extract

20 x 20 x 5cm baking tray, oiled
 or buttered

Place the potato in a pan of boiling water and boil until just tender,
about 12–15 minutes depending on its size. Drain and return to the pan.
Cover the pan with a clean tea towel to absorb the steam – you don't
want sloshy spuds for this recipe.

Leave to cool then mash the potato until silky smooth. Use a stick blender
if you have one.

Add the vanilla extract and, a little at a time, mix in the icing sugar until
you have a firm dough. It's unlikely to taste of potato whatsoever at this
point but taste it, and if necessary, add more sugar.

Press into the tray and leave to set for an hour before cutting into bars of
about 10 x 4cm. Keep cool in the fridge.

Toast the coconut in a frying pan over a gentle heat, stirring constantly
to avoid burning. Spread a third of the coconut on to a sheet of greaseproof paper.

Melt the chocolate in a bowl set over a pan of simmering water, making
sure the bottom of the bowl does not touch the water. Remove the macaroon bars from the fridge and dip each bar in the melted chocolate to
coat thoroughly, then place on the sheet of coconut. Sprinkle with the

remaining coconut to coat the top of the bars then leave to set. Kept refrigerated in a container, the bars will last for up to 2 weeks.

MACKINTOSH'S SPECIAL TOFFEE
Halifax

Many of our greatest British sweet manufacturers were founded by unique individuals. The following piece of colourful prose was written, as an advertising bill, by one such character when he and his 'special toffees' made their grand entrance into the United States of America:

'I am John Mackintosh, the Toffee King, Sovereign of Pleasure, Emperor of Joy. My old English candy tickles my millions of subjects. My Court Jester's name is Appetite. I was crowned by the lovers of good things to eat. My most loyal subjects are dear little children. My throne is guarded by the Imperial Unarmed Army of Candy Makers. I am the world's largest consumer of butter, my own herd of prize cattle graze the Yorkshire hills. I buy sugar by the trainload. I am John Mackintosh, Toffee King of England, and I rule alone.'

John Mackintosh wasn't actually a confectioner at all. According to renowned Welsh confectioner Stephen Bray, Mackintosh bought the recipe for his 'special toffees' from one of Bray's ancestor's for a fiver and when he and his wife Violet pitched their savings into a small pastry shop in Halifax in 1890 the idea was that Violet would run the shop whilst John continued with his day job at the cotton mill. It was the smooth and creamy 'special' toffee, a different kind of sweet to the usual hard, brittle-textured stuff that propelled the couple to international fame. Just nine years after they opened their pastry shop, John and Violet

Mackintosh became a limited company and in 1904 the enterprising John set up business in America (later in Germany, Canada and Australia as well), employing a thousand people. John died in 1920 but the company stayed in the family and merged with fellow UK confectioners, Rowntree, in 1969. In 1988, Rowntree Mackintosh was taken over by Nestlé, which marked the end of a great British sweet-making era. Nestlé's version of the toffee can, of course, still be bought.

MARS BAR
Slough

For many people, the Berkshire town of Slough is synonymous with the Mars Bar, since that is where it has been made since 1932. But this great British chocolate was actually invented in 1924 by an American, Frank C. Mars (and later adapted by his son Forrest) in a deliberate effort to topple the Hershey Bar as America's top chocolate treat. I've claimed it for Britain because manufacturing began, and has only ever been, here. Mars Senior had the idea to turn the popular malted milk drinks, full of goodness and beloved by his country, into a confection that could be marketed as a proper, nutritious treat. Clever. And indeed, despite all its sugar and high calorific value, the Mars bar has in the past been advertised as good for us. Who remembers the advertising jingle 'A Mars A Day Helps You Work, Rest and Play'? (What you are less likely to remember is the short-lived pineapple-flavoured Mars bar that bit the dust almost as soon as it rolled off the factory lines.)

There are conflicting stories of what happened between Forrest and his father Frank. Apparently, father and son had been separated since Forrest was just five years old, but were reunited when he had a run-in with the law at the age of 18. After bailing him out, Frank offered his son a position in his confectionery company, which was just beginning to do well. But Forrest was ambitious and had ideas of his own. After one conflict too many, Forrest was booted out and moved to Europe.

After lowly jobs at both Tobler and Nestlé where the young man gleaned what information he could without divulging the fact that he had a keen interest in chocolate, Forrest moved to England in 1932 and found affordable factory premises in Slough. Forrest's first project was to perfect his father's Milky Way (which was originally invented by Frank to rival the Hershey Bar) by turning it into the Mars bar. He also 'invented' a new Milky Way for the British market and coined the slogan 'The sweet you can eat between meals'. Some 80 years later and the Mars bar is still going strong, but has diminished not only in size (the thickness of the chocolate has been reduced and the nougat is lighter, more aerated and, indeed, easier to chew), but in calorific value. The 'old' Mars bar had 365 calories; the new one, available since 2002, has 260 … Unless you cover it in batter and deep-fry it, of course, but that's a whole other story.

Mars Bar Brownies

Makes 16 square brownies

100g unsalted butter
40g cocoa powder, sifted
2 eggs, loosely beaten
200g caster sugar
50g self-raising flour, sifted
a couple of drops of orange, vanilla or hazelnut essence (optional)
100g Mars bar, roughly chopped into 1cm cubes

crème fraîche, whipped cream or ice cream, to serve
raspberries, to serve

20 x 20 x 5cm cake tin, buttered and lined with non-stick baking paper

Preheat the oven to 180°C/gas mark 4.

In a small pan, melt the butter, remove from the heat and then stir in the sifted cocoa powder until you have a smooth mixture. Leave to cool.

Whisk together the eggs and sugar until fluffy and bubbly. Add the cooled butter/cocoa mixture, then sift the flour on top and stir in gently with a wooden spoon. If you want to add essence, now's the time. Fold in the Mars, then pour the mix into the lined tin. At this stage you might think that the mixture looks a little thin but it will rise beautifully. Bake for about 25 minutes until the top is beginning to crisp slightly and the brownie has shrunk a little from the sides of the tin. Leave the tin to cool completely on a wire rack otherwise the brownies won't hold their shape. Cut into squares and serve with crème fraîche and raspberries.

Did you know?
It was because of a Mars bar that chocolate ended up being one of the substances banned by the Jockey Club. It isn't jockeys that are forbidden from munching on a bar prior to a race, but the horse. It was at Ascot that the jockey of a winning horse, called Tied Cottage, was grassed on by a rival who had seen the jockey feed his winning steed a Mars bar. The theobromine in the chocolate was suspected of giving the animal the extra oomph needed to win the race, hence the ban by the Club.

MEALIE CANDY

It's fair to say that Scots are known for having a sweet tooth. It's also fair to say that they're known for eating lots of porridge. Too much sugar can cause dental caries, heart disease, obesity and diabetes (or all four), whereas oats are dubbed a superfood: not only do they give a stable, slow release of energy, but they also scour the cholesterol from our arteries. This sweet happily combines the devil on the shoulder (sugar) with the angel on the other (oats) so, you might say, mealie candy is the perfectly balanced snack.

250g granulated white sugar
75g treacle or golden syrup
100ml water
40g oatmeal, toasted

1 tsp ground ginger

12cm x 10cm shallow tray or tub,
lined with parchment paper

Preheat the oven to 100°C/gas mark ¼.

Place the oatmeal in a baking dish in the oven to warm.

Put the sugar, treacle and water in a large heavy-bottomed pan. Bring to the boil and cook steadily for 10 minutes. Remove from the heat and beat until creamy. Thoroughly stir in the warmed oatmeal and ginger, then immediately pour into the tin and, when cool enough, mark into squares.

NOUGAT (CWNFFETS)
Wales

Although the word 'nougat' has French origins, the sweet itself has been claimed by Italy (where it's called torrone) and Spain (turrón). Some records even state that it came from Ancient Egypt or, more vaguely, 'the Orient'. However, there's a medieval Welsh recipe for 'cwnffets' that is remarkably similar to nougat, and so in the absence of any definitive evidence to the contrary I'd like to set the cat amongst the pigeons and claim it for Wales. Author Bobby Freeman's First Catch Your Peacock, *a guide to Welsh food and food history reproduces a medieval recipe for 'cwnffets' which first appeared in the 1976 publication* Bwyd y Beirdd (Food of the Bards 1350—1650) *by Enid Roberts. The recipe for 'cwnffets' – a rich, chewy sweet, stuffed with fruit and nuts – is simple, and in making it you end up with something very like nougat, also a chewy concoction which contains hot syrup or honey folded into egg whites with the addition of nuts and/or fruit, often with the addition of rice paper on the top and bottom. Really, the only difference here is in the name and the addition of ginger/rice paper – so Welsh it shall be.*

420g caster sugar

100g liquid glucose

2 large egg whites

450g raisins, hazelnuts, almonds, chopped figs, glacé cherries … warmed in a low oven

1 tsp ground ginger

125g clear runny honey

100g icing sugar

20 x 20 x 5cm tray, lined with rice paper

machine whisk

Line the baking tray with rice paper.

Combine 400g sugar and glucose in a heavy-bottomed pan, attaching your sugar thermometer to the inside of the pan. Stir over a very low heat until the mixture reaches 145°C, remove from the heat and take out the thermometer.

Whisk the egg whites with 20g sugar in a large heatproof bowl to stiff peaks, then pour over the honey. Slowly add the hot sugar and glucose to the egg whites, continue to whisk until just stiff and glossy. Fold in the mixed fruits and nuts and the ginger. Scoop the mixture into the lined tray and press a sheet of rice paper on top and weight it. Leave to set overnight. Cut or break into squares and dust with icing sugar.

NUTTY NUBS
Newport, South Wales

Also called nutty nibs, nutty nubs are a buttery nut brittle, bashed into a rustic-looking heap of nutty rubble, invented by the Bray family from South Wales. The Brays are famous for having sold the recipe for a very 'special toffee' to John Mackintosh (see page 119), and also for supplying Winston Churchill with his favourite Welsh mints. What sets nutty nubs apart from traditional brittles is that salted peanuts are used in the recipe, something you won't find in traditional versions, which are only made with plain nuts. The sweets are easy to make at home, and deliciously moreish. They make a great ice cream topping!

100g golden caster sugar
50g assorted unsalted nuts
   (cashews, macadamia, hazelnut
   and brazil nuts), warmed in a
   low oven and roughly chopped

50g salted peanuts, roughly
   chopped
a couple of drops of vanilla essence

32 x 22cm shallow baking tray,
   buttered
toffee hammer

Place the sugar in a medium-sized heavy-bottomed pan and cook over a low heat, swirling the pan gently so the sugar browns evenly. As the sugar heats it will start to caramelise; this is a slow process. Once the sugar has darkened, immediately remove the pan from the heat, tip in the warmed nuts and add the vanilla essence. Pour into the baking tray and set aside.

Once cool, use a toffee hammer to break into small pieces. You can leave as larger shards if you like, which are really a nut brittle, but nubs are small and … err … nub-like.

PARMA VIOLETS

PARMA VIOLETS

Parma Violets belong to a group of delicately-flavoured sweets called floral cachous. The 'cachou' is a breath-freshening sweet and has its origins in the Indian custom of crunching up tiny sugared aniseeds after a spicy meal. Swizzels Matlow first launched the sweets in the 1930s and they are still popular today. The lovely, powdery texture of the little lilac-coloured discs pairs wonderfully with the sweet, floral flavour – perfect for freshening the breath. When Swizzels Matlow threatened to alter the recipe a few years ago, there was such an uproar that they changed their minds. It would be folly to try to replicate the Parma Violet sweet at home as you'd need specialised equipment to compress the little discs. However, if you're making icing to go on top of a cake, try grinding some into the icing sugar to give a little twist to the flavour. You might also like to try the following recipe.

Parma Violet Cupcakes

Makes 12

150g self-raising flour
125g plain flour
100g unsalted butter, at room
   temperature
225g caster sugar
   (golden or white)
2 large eggs, loosely beaten
120ml milk
¼ tsp violet flavouring or extract

3 x packets small Parma Violets,
   ground to a powder, plus extra
   sweets to decorate
600ml whipping cream
purple sugar flowers, to decorate
   (optional)

deep 12-hole muffin tray, lined with
   muffin cases

Preheat the oven to 180°C/gas mark 4.

Sift the flours together in a bowl and set to one side. In a separate bowl, cream the butter and sugar until fluffy. Add the eggs a little at a time, stirring well. Add a spoonful of flour with the last of the egg, so that the mixture doesn't curdle.

Measure the milk into a jug and stir in the violet essence. Add the flour and the milk to the egg mixture, alternating between the two and mixing well.

When thoroughly combined, spoon the mixture equally into the cases and bake for 25 minutes, turning halfway through. Check they're done by inserting a skewer into the centre of a cake – it should come out clean. Leave to cool completely on a wire rack before decorating.

Add the ground Parma Violets to the cream, then whip until stiff. Transfer to a piping bag and pipe on to the cupcakes using a medium nozzle, then stud the cream with more Parma Violets and purple-coloured icing flowers.

Did you know?
You can also make Parma Violet-flavoured vodka. Add 4 packs of the small sweets to a 1-litre bottle of vodka. After only a day the flavour will have infused to give an interesting, unusual liquor. Shake before serving to disperse the froth which will have accumulated at the top of the bottle.

PEAR DROPS
Oswaldtwhistle

Stockleys factory in the town of Oswaldtwhistle in Lancashire (makers of Coltsfoot rock, see page 74) is also the home of the world's largest pear drop, which is 1.7m tall and weighs 584.23kg. It is kept behind lock and key in a glass cabinet, like a religious relic, admired by keen sweetie pilgrims. Pear drops are boiled sweets, coloured half red half yellow, and unsurprisingly, they're shaped like a pear. Stockleys use only natural flavourings for its pear drops, but you may detect a certain acrid varnish-y tang in those made by other brands. This is because the pear flavouring is provided by a chemical called isoamyl acetate, which is actually also used in some varnishes!

This recipe uses real pear juice and the sweets will be one colour so will not look exactly like the usual pink and yellow ones.

450g caster sugar
50ml water
175ml fresh pear juice
¼ tsp cream of tartar
30ml lemon juice
2 drops yellow food colouring
4 drops pear flavouring (optional)

50g white caster sugar, ground in a blender, for coating (put the sugar into a deep bowl to avoid covering everything with a fine sugary dust)

38 x 30cm shallow baking tray, oiled

Fill a bowl large enough to hold your pan, with water. The kitchen sink will do if you don't have a big enough bowl.

Put the sugar, water, 150ml of the pear juice and the cream of tartar into a heavy-bottomed pan, attaching your sugar thermometer to the pan. Heat gently until the sugar has completely dissolved. Turn up the heat and cook until your sugar thermometer reads 114°C (soft ball stage).

PEAR DROPS
Oswaldtwhistle

Remove from the heat and add the remaining pear juice, lemon juice and the food colouring. Don't stir. Put the pan back on the heat and boil again until the mixture reaches 154°C (hard crack stage).

Remove the pan from the heat immediately and rest in the cold water for a minute or so to arrest the cooking.

Pour the mixture on to the tray and, when it is cool enough to handle, pull into long ropes. Snip off 2.5cm lengths and roll each into a pear-drop shape. Before completely hard, roll each pear drop in the extra ground caster sugar.

PEGGY'S LEG
Letterkenny, Ireland

Peggy's leg is said to be the first Irish stick of rock, golden in colour and flavoured with caramel rather than mint, which is common to English rock. It was developed by Oatfields in Letterkenny and bore a wrapper that read 'Peggy's Leg That Never Wore A Garter!' Although the factory closed down in 2012, the good news – for all those of you who are now gasping at the memory of the Peggy's leg – is that yes, it is still being made, and it is still available. Athlone Sweets re-introduced Peggy's leg, and can't make enough of the stuff. You can buy it from them online. If you'd prefer to make your own Peggy's leg, replace the peppermint in a recipe for 'seaside' rock (see page 139) with caramel flavouring.

Incidentally, Peggy's Leg is also the name of a hairy Irish classic folk/rock band that lurked around the music scene in Ireland between 1972 and 1975. Presumably named after the sweet, the band were famed for their interpretations of pieces by famous classical composers.

PEPPERMINT CREAMS

Their set included a 'demented' interpretation of the Willam Tell overture. I'd like to hear that.

PEPPERMINT CREAMS

Peppermint creams have been claimed by Scotland, the Lake District, Yorkshire, the South East ... just about everywhere. The truth is, we just don't know how, or where, this Victorian delicacy was first concocted. Peppermint creams are commercially available in many forms. They all follow the same idea: a basic peppermint-flavoured fondant, sometimes stiff and sometimes gooey, and sometimes encased in chocolate (plain or milk, although plain tends to work better with the sharpness of the mint). Mint itself was originally used as both a breath-freshener and as a digestif, hence the creams are often served up after dinner.

You can, if you like, buy very posh peppermint creams, but no matter how fancy the packaging nothing compares to fresh, home-made ones. What's more they are a doddle to make. The method here also has the advantage of needing no cooking whatsoever. The sweets will take a day to dry out, so plan accordingly.

2 medium egg whites
450g icing sugar, plus a little extra
   for dusting

6 drops peppermint essence or oil,
   or to taste
food colouring (optional)
dark chocolate, melted (optional)

Whisk the egg whites in a large bowl until frothy. Sift the icing sugar into the egg whites, a little at a time, stirring thoroughly as you go. The idea is to make a stiff but smooth mixture so, depending on the size of the eggs, you may not need all of the icing sugar. Add the peppermint flavouring and food colouring, if using. You may need to add a little more icing sugar to soak up the excess liquid. Knead the mixture until you have a smooth paste.

The traditional way to make peppermint creams is to make balls and then flatten them into fattish discs about the size of a 10-pence piece. Make grooves in them with the tines of a fork.

Leave on greaseproof paper to dry out for 24 hours, at which point you can half-dip them in melted chocolate if the fancy takes you.

POLO MINTS
York

Did you know that if you smash a Polo in a darkened room with a hammer, you'll see sparks of light? This is a phenomenon known as 'triboluminescence', caused by the friction of the two surfaces meeting. You can produce the same effect when pulling open self-seal envelopes in the dark.

Polos, the white mint-flavoured sweet shaped like a lifebelt, came along in 1939, towards the end of what would prove to be a period of great creativity for Rowntree of York, inspired in no small part by the friendly rivalry between one of Rowntree's directors, George Harris, with Forrest Mars, the genius behind (among other sweets) the Mars bar. The mints themselves, with their name raised around the edge of the hoop, are pressed with a force equivalent to that of two elephants jumping up and down on them.

My gran refused to eat Polos, protesting that she didn't see the point of paying for the air in the middle. She preferred her mints to be solid; better value for money, she said.

According to Nestlé, Polos are the UK's most popular mint. Over 20 million mints are manufactured every year, with 150 consumed every second. Incidentally, there's no recipe here since the Polo mint is beyond the capability of the domestic kitchen.

RILEY'S BRIDGEND TOFFEE
Bridgend, South Wales

In an unassuming little town in South Wales I discovered a story whose plotline is just made for the cinema. It features two women, separated by a generation, each with the same steely streak of determination coursing through their veins. Having ladies involved in sweets at all is unusual; most of the entrepreneurs are men.

In 1907, Fred Riley and his brother J.H. established a confectionery manufacturing business in Halifax. Their most sought-after product was their amazing chocolate toffee rolls, which at the time came in several flavours as well as the original creamy toffee. The recipe was in fact written down by Fred and J.H.'s niece, Ella, who put the handwritten recipe in between the pages of a cookery book. The little piece of paper was forgotten about for several decades...

Riley's grew fast, and in 1911 it moved production to new premises, whose factory chimney had the Riley's name picked out in letters over two metres high. And the toffee rolls, renowned for their high quality and delicious flavour, streamed out across the nation.

In 1953, J.H. Riley died and Riley's was bought out by another renowned British confectionery company, Nuttalls, before later being bought by the Kraft corporation where its name languished on the shelves, abandoned.

Ella's granddaughter Freya inherited that old recipe book and one day, flicking though it, she came across the recipe for Riley's toffee rolls. Freya followed the recipe and discovered that the end result was absolutely delicious. Soon, she and her husband Steve could hardly keep up with the demand from their family and friends and decided it would be a good idea to sell the sweets under Freya's family name, in honour of Ella. This idea met its match when Freya realised that Kraft actually owned the rights to her family name and brand. Knowing that there was no way an individual would be able to take on a gigantic organisation, Freya nevertheless took legal advice and found that she had a chance of claiming back her heritage. With registered names or brands, there's a 'use it or lose it' policy and luckily the Riley's name was due for renewal about a year after Freya began her investigations. It must have been a tense wait on the day that renewal was due; but at midnight, the name became free and Freya and Steve claimed it immediately.

Ella Riley's Chocolate Toffee Rolls, made in the kitchen behind Steve and Freya's shop in Bridgend, South Wales, are now supplied to over 157 outlets, including their first American buyer. Although they will never divulge the recipe for the rolls, Steve and Freya very kindly gave me the recipe for a toffee that they make in honour of Bridgend's football and rugby teams, which both use yellow and blue as their colours. Freya and Steve sell large quantities of this toffee and have adapted the recipe for domestic use. The amount here is still quite significant but the end result is so delicious that you won't regret having lots of it!

Makes approx 1kg

225g golden syrup
500g caster sugar
90ml water
2 tsp vanilla extract
2.4kg white chocolate

good pinch of blue powder food colouring (NB liquid colouring won't work with chocolate)

32 x 22cm baking tray, lined with greaseproof paper

Fill a sink or heatproof bowl, large enough to hold your pan, with cold water. Put all the ingredients except the chocolate and colouring into a heavy-bottomed pan. Melt over a low heat, stirring until everything has dissolved. Increase the heat and bring to the boil without stirring until the mixture turns a pale, egg-yolk yellow in colour and reaches 130°C, then remove the pan from the heat. If the mixture is turning a little too brown, plunge the bottom of the pan immediately into the cold water to stop the cooking.

Pour the toffee on to the lined tray. Leave for a few hours in a cool place until the toffee has set completely

When the toffee is set, break 1kg of the white chocolate into a heatproof bowl set over a pan of simmering water and leave to melt. (Alternatively, do this in a microwave on a low heat, stopping and stirring every 30 seconds.) Add a further 200g white chocolate to the melted chocolate and allow this to melt to temper the chocolate (for more information about this, see page 19).

Spread the chocolate as evenly as you can on top of the toffee (if you're better at a rustic style of spreading, believe me, no one will complain). Leave to set.

Once set, turn out on to a sheet of greaseproof paper and remove the paper on the bottom on the toffee. Repeat the process with the rest of the chocolate. Once melted thoroughly, add the blue food colouring powder, stirring well. Spread the blue chocolate on to the bare side of the toffee and leave to set. Break into pieces.

ROCK (THE SEASIDE STUFF)
Morecambe (possibly)

ROCK (THE SEASIDE STUFF)
Morecambe (possibly)

'A fellow took my photograph, it cost one and three.
I said when it was done, "Is that supposed to be me?
You've properly mucked it up – the only thing I can see
Is my little stick of Blackpool rock."'

Blackpool Rock, George Formby, 1937

As a souvenir of a trip to the coast, a stick of rock – the solid tubes of candy, often flavoured with peppermint – is an absolute must – whether you actually like eating the stuff or not. For a factory worker in the nineteenth and early part of the twentieth century, a visit to the seaside was as close as he or she would get to a holiday, and a stick of rock proved the perfect souvenir of the day – cheap, fun and complete with a picture of the destination, as well as the name of it running through its core. But the real heyday for sticks of rock coincided with that of the seaside resort. In the 1950s and 60s, the working man and his family had a bit of cash to spare for such jaunts but had not yet been lured away from the British seaside by the temptations of cheap flights and holidays to Spain.

The process of making lettered rock is a collision of ingenuity and industry, and something that's probably beyond the realm of most domestic kitchens. A large quantity of sugar and glucose is boiled until it reaches a temperature of approximately 146°C (hard crack stage). Some of the resulting gloop is coloured (red for the lettering, usually) and flavoured (traditionally with mint) and poured on to a huge table. It is then cooled until it can be placed on to a mechanical 'pulling' machine where it is stretched and pulled by means of rotating arms until it acquires that familiar silky sheen. As the main body of the rock is white, the red letters are constructed rather like digital letters, with red strips, which are placed along the body of white sugar. Once this tricky work is done, the red and white lump is rolled into a cylinder and then coated with an external layer of coloured pulled sugar. At this point the whole shebang is a huge, heavy and cumbersome mass – extremely wide and long. It is pulled further to stretch it to an acceptable narrowness and then snipped into regular lengths. The messages that can be inserted into rock are limited only by space and the imagination.

There are several individuals who lay claim to the invention of sea-side rock but my favourite is Dick Taylor, aka Dynamite Dick, from Morecambe. The story goes that Dick had been a part of the Klondike gold rush before he returned to his home town and invented rock. His nickname was apt for two reasons; for his glamorous gold-mining activities, which would have required lots of exciting explosions, and because a stick of rock does, in fact, resemble a stick of dynamite. Dick Taylor also made a confection that was known as TNT, or 'Taylor's Noted Toffee'. If Dick really had been a part of the Klondike gold rush, then his rock would have first exploded on to the streets of Morecambe any time between 1896 and 1914. The argument is likely to rage on for some time, though.

SHERBET
London

Although we might think of sherbet either as the fizzy powder that comes in packets with a liquorice stick to dip (a sherbet fountain) or a lollipop (a sherbet dib dab), or as the filling of a flying saucer, its origins are, in fact, considerably more exotic. The word sherbet derives from the Arabic verb, shariba, meaning 'to drink', which is also the origin of 'sorbet' and 'syrup'. Sherbet, or sharbat, is also an Arabian iced drink, made from fruit, sugar and vinegar – it must be deliciously refreshing in the arid heat

SHERBET

London

of the Arabian desert. Arabian sherbet is flavoured with all sorts of things: rose petals, mint, various kinds of fruit (in particular, lemons), spices, even vinegar – not to be confused with today's chip-shop vinegar, rather a fermented wine or juice – and also verjuice, the juice of sour grapes.

The first evidence we have of the arrival of sherbet in Britain is an advertisement, dated 1662, for the 'Great Turk Coffee House' in Exchange Alley in London. As well as tea, coffee and tobacco, customers could enjoy chocolate and a variety of sherbet drinks '… made in Turkie, of lemons, roses, and violets perfumed'.

If you love both sherbet and liquorice, sweets don't get much better than flyers. These are a hollow tube of liquorice packed with sherbet and sealed with a solid plug of sherbet at the end. You bite the end, throw your head back and pour the rest of the fizzy crystals into your mouth.

The best sherbet I have ever tasted was made by Karl Cheetham, chef at the Gliffaes Country House Hotel just outside Crickhowell in Wales. Karl flavours his with freeze-dried plump, sweet raspberries that were picked from just outside the door. I've used a simpler, but just as delicious, method in this recipe.

¼ tsp citric acid
¼ tsp tartaric acid
¾ tsp bicarbonate of soda
6 heaped tbsp finest-textured caster sugar you can find

5 drops fruit essence (orange, lemon, lime, blackcurrant – whatever you prefer)
a drop of the appropriate food colouring (optional)

Simply put the first three ingredients into a bowl and crush together with the back of a spoon to remove any lumps. Then blend the sugar to make it even finer (some recipes call for icing sugar but this tends to lump). Add the sugar to the bicarb mix, add the flavouring and colouring and stir thoroughly.

Spread thinly on to greaseproof paper and leave to dry out completely. This will take up to a couple of hours so keep checking it. Transfer to an airtight container. Kept like this, the sherbet will last for a month. If it clumps together, spread on a baking sheet and heat in a low oven for 10 minutes then dry out again, as above.

SMARTIES
York

The Smarties of my childhood came in a colourful cardboard tube with a plastic pop-off lid; the underside of the lid had a letter on it, useful for all sorts of things, none of which I can actually think of, but still lovely, and an enticing little bonus of the sort that kids adore. I liked the orange ones best. The problem was, so did my dad. So I used to pinch our favourites out of the tube, suck the orange off them until they were white, optimistically try to dry them out, and then put them back in the tube. I knew how to rock it in the 1970s.

Rowntree in York had been making the chocolate niblet bean, as it was then known, since the 1880s, then in 1937 the bean was reborn as the Smartie. And, as they say, the rest is history. The iconic chocolate discs, with a convex curve to each side, coated in a crisp sugar shell have been popular ever since.

When the Hexatubes were introduced in 2005, the nation rose up and expressed its dudgeon by means of online forums, petitions and angry letters to both newspapers and to Smarties HQ. However Smarties prevailed and the hexatubes have stuck. Today Smarties are truly global, with gazillions of the tantalising, colourful little beans jumping into the hexagonal tubes and into the hands of happy customers across the world. Or on to yummy cookies like these.

SMARTIES
York

Smartie Cookies

Makes about 20 very large cookies

350g plain flour
1 tsp bicarbonate of soda
1 tsp baking powder
300g caster sugar
1 medium egg, beaten
1 tsp vanilla extract
250g butter, softened, plus extra for greasing.

a pinch of salt
300g Smarties (260g for the cake, 40g for 'testing')

two 38 x 30cm baking trays, buttered

Preheat the oven to 180°C/gas mark 4.

Sift together the flour, bicarbonate of soda and baking powder. In a separate bowl, cream together the butter and sugar until fluffy and gorgeous, then beat in the vanilla extract and egg.

Gradually sift in the flour until you have a stiff dough, then divide the dough into 20 balls (or fewer if you want trendy gigantic cookies). Flatten the balls into circles then stud with Smarties and place on the buttered baking trays. The cookies spread as they bake so allow them plenty of room to manoeuvre.

Bake for 15 minutes. The cookies should be golden brown, the jewel-colours of the Smarties peeking through. Leave to cool on a wire rack before eating, and store in airtight jars for up to 2 weeks.

SOOR PLOOMS
Galashiels and Peebles

SOOR PLOOMS
Galashiels and Peebles

I remember the first and last time I had a soor ploom. I was offered the dayglo nuclear acid green ball by someone I met while drifting down the Caledonian Canal in a small dog-grade cruiser. It seemed a good idea at the time, but after a few seconds of sucking the sweet I felt as though the insides of my mouth were turning inside out, and all moisture was being drained from my body. As a sweet the soor ploom is wasted; as a weapon of war it would fare much better. But don't let me put you off.

Those good citizens north of the English border consume more sugar per capita than anyone else in the UK, and have wide and varied ways of accessing the sweet stuff, so, if I'm honest, the popularity of the soor ploom from Galashiels is something of a mystery to me.

The Galashiels coat of arms features two foxes reaching up to eat plums from a tree, under which is the motto 'Sour Plums'. It commemorates an incident that happened in 1337 when the English king, Edward III, was invading Scotland. A party of English soldiers had established themselves in Galashiels. The story goes that the soldiers decided to wander in the woods to look for something to eat. Apparently they were seeking wild plums. Whether or not they found any is unknown – perhaps they found damsons or sloes, which have the same effect on the palate as the latter-day soor ploom – but in any case, a party of Scots discovered their enemy, swore that they would give them more 'soor plooms' than they'd bargained for and drove them into the banks of the River Tweed, slaughtering the lot of them. Perhaps the foxes on the coat of arms represent the English?

I haven't included a specific recipe here; however, if you want to try making your own soor plooms, take the basic Pulled Toffee Recipe (see page 32) and add a generous pinch of malic acid for a mouth-puckering punch of a sweet.

SUGARED ALMONDS

Sugared almonds – the pretty, pastel-coloured coated nuts – are perhaps most commonly associated with wedding favours, where they are presented to the recipient tied up in a little bag or box. Almonds, in common with other nuts, represent fertility. And if you've ever noticed there are usually five, that's because this number represents longevity, fertility, wealth, health and happiness. Prior to the ready availability of sugar, the almonds were coated in honey and were known as 'confetti', from the word 'confit' (a sweet with something inside, such as gobstoppers, Smarties and liquorice torpedoes). Although these traditions have their origins in Italy rather than in Great Britain, our enthusiasm for them justifies them being included here. The recipe here will not make the very slick almonds that are produced on a commercial basis – the rolling machines needed are just not practical for domestic use – but you won't be disappointed with the home-made kind.

175g large blanched almonds
450g granulated sugar
150ml water

pinch of cream of tartar
4 drops of liquid food colouring
   (optional)

Place the almonds in a single layer in an ovenproof dish with a lid (Pyrex is fine) and put in a very low oven (110°C/gas mark ¼) to warm.

Put the sugar, water and cream of tartar into a heavy-bottomed saucepan, attaching your sugar thermometer to the inside of the pan, and stir over a low heat to dissolve the sugar completely. Bring to the boil and continue boiling until the mixture hits 116°C.

Scoop off any scum that rises to the surface, and add the colouring, if using. Add more food colouring for a deeper colour, if preferred.

Take the nuts out of the oven and carefully pour some of the sugar over them, turning them with a palette knife to coat. Let the sugar set (about 10 minutes) then bring the sugar back to the boil and repeat the coating process until all the sugar is used up – you will need about 3 coats. Store your sugared almonds for up to two weeks in an airtight container.

TABLET
Scotland

Die-hard of bring-and-buy sales everywhere, but particularly in Scotland whence is originates, tablet might sound like a humble little sweet; however, it should not be underestimated. It's a soft, incredibly sweet confection, like a very sugary piece of fudge where you can almost feel yourself biting into the sugar granules. Sometimes it's flavoured. Tablet is absolutely delicious, albeit in small doses. Try it with a stern cup of coffee after dinner, which lends it a rather sophisticated air.

450g granulated white sugar
100g unsalted butter
150ml milk
150ml water

200ml condensed milk
1 tsp vanilla extract or other
 flavouring (see below)

For a chunky tablet, butter a 20 x 20 x 5cm baking tin; if you prefer a slimmer tablet, choose a larger vessel. Line with non-stick baking paper and set to one side.

Put all the ingredients, except for the condensed milk and the flavouring, into a heavy-bottomed pan, attaching your sugar thermometer to the inside. Over a low heat, stir gently until the sugar has dissolved. Bring to the boil and heat to 114°C (soft ball stage), then remove from the heat

TABLET
Scotland

immediately and stir in the condensed milk. Return to the heat and continue to cook to 116°C (on the edge between soft ball and firm ball stage), stirring occasionally to ensure that the mixture browns evenly. Take the pan off the stove, leave for a few minutes to cool down, then add your flavouring.

A good tablet is all about the next part. Stir the mixture briskly with a wooden spoon until the colour lightens and the texture becomes creamy. This should take about 3 minutes (the cooler the kitchen, the quicker the process). Pour the resulting mix into the buttered tin and, once it has cooled but is still soft, cut into squares.

A Note on Flavourings
Chocolate works well – add in a handful of chocolate chips and let them make streaks through the mixture just before pouring into the tray. You might try rose essence, too. Minty flavours, in my opinion, don't sit well with tablet, although mint is a popular flavour in Scotland ,so it's just a matter of taste. What does work very well, however, it being a Scottish recipe, is a generous glug of whisky. By the way, it's important to add the flavouring once the mixture is off the stove, otherwise the heat will make it fizzle away to nothing.

Brechin Tablet

When I was researching tablet a friend tipped me off about a story that had appeared in the Brechin Advertiser, *which related that a local chap, Alistair Morgan, had found an obscure recipe for a kind of tablet indigenous to Brechin. The tablet contained cherries and walnuts. Alistair fancied reviving the recipe of his hometown but couldn't find much more information.*

As it happened, I, too, own a copy of the book that Alistair mentioned, and I, too, had wondered about the origins of Brechin tablet. I spoke to the book's author, Carol Wilson, a renowned food historian, who told me that the original recipe had been found in an ancient and tattered book no longer in print. Then I called Alistair. He believes that Brechin tablet is something that the town should celebrate, so he set up a small company, making it and distributing it himself. I do hope his plan succeeds.

My conversation with Alistair got me thinking. The addition of walnuts to the tablet recipe, in the days before supermarkets and lorry loads of produce made their way from one part of the country to another, must have meant that there was an abundance of walnuts in the Brechin area itself, as well as a decent crop of cherries, which are also key to the recipe. I discovered that there are, indeed, walnut trees in the area. Not only that, but coincidentally, the Angus Orchards Project, as well as planting apple trees, are planting both cherry and walnut trees in the area as part of their programme … Such information gives me goosebumps. Perhaps walnut and cherry was chosen by someone, somewhere, in homage to the recipe? I do hope so.

450g caster sugar
300ml single cream
1 tbsp golden syrup
100g blanched walnuts (the husks
  leave a bitter taste), chopped
25g red glacé cherries, chopped

25g green glacé cherries, angelica
  or candied peel, chopped
1 tsp vanilla extract

20 x 20 x 5cm baking tin, buttered

In a heavy-bottomed pan, with your sugar thermometer attached to the inside, heat the sugar and cream very gently until the sugar has dissolved, taking care that the cream does not scorch. Add the syrup and stir until the mixture just starts to boil. Remove from the heat and add the walnuts and fruit, stirring well. Return to the stove and heat the mixture to 116 °C. Remove from the heat and stir in the vanilla extract. Leave to cool for a few minutes, then beat briskly with a wooden spoon until the texture becomes grainy and the colour lightens. Once this stage is reached, quickly pour into the tin, and, when your tablet has solidified sufficiently, cut into squares.

TAFFI TRIOG
North Wales

Another traditional Welsh confection, taffi triog translates as treacle toffee and this particular type of treat is the North Welsh version of South Wales' Loshin Du, or black sweet (see page 112). Taffi triog uses more in the way of ingredients and has a milder taste; it's not quite so intense on the treacle.

450g demerara sugar
150ml water
120g unsalted butter
  ¼ tsp cream of tartar
  3 tbsp black treacle

3 tbsp golden syrup
2 drops of vinegar

20 x 20cm shallow baking tray, buttered

Put the sugar in a heavy-bottomed saucepan, attach your sugar thermometer to the inside of the pan, then add the water. Stir continually over a low heat until the sugar has dissolved, then add all the other ingredients. Still stirring, bring the mixture to the boil and boil steadily until the thermometer reaches 131°C (just beyond hard ball stage). Pour the mixture into the tray and mark into squares when cool.

TAFFI TWM
Tregaron, Wales

Unless you live in Wales, the name Twm Sion Cati (pronounced 'tum shon catti') probably won't mean anything to you, but in short, the easiest way to describe Robin Hood is to call him the English Twm Sion Cati.

Like Robin Hood, it wasn't so much what Twm did but the way that he did it that made people love him, and like Robin, he stole from the rich in order to redistribute the wealth to the poor. This rogueish rebel had such swagger and brash wit that even the people he robbed felt as though he was doing them a favour. There are numerous accounts of his exploits and in one tale he even ends up in the respectable position of mayor of Brecon! Added to this reputation is a dash of wizardry as well as skills as a poet.

Visible evidence of Twm's legend is scant, but hidden perilously high up on Dinas Hill is Twm Sion Cati's cave where it's said he holed up during dangerous times.

Today, Twm is celebrated in Wales every year on May 17th, and this boozy toffee recipe is made in his honour. The recipe below is courtesy of the great Hazel Thomas, the first female chef to be employed by Anton Mosimann. Hazel's taffi twm requires a generous dash of Penderyn Welsh whisky. She uses molasses, which makes for a more complex flavour than granulated white sugar, and is packed full of minerals making it more nutritious (!).

200g molasses sugar
200g black treacle
50g unsalted Welsh (or other)
    butter, plus extra for greasing

1 tbsp Penderyn whisky

20 x 20cm shallow baking tray, buttered

Tip all the ingredients except the whisky into a heavy-bottomed pan, attaching your sugar thermometer to the inside. Heat gently until everything has melted and the mixture starts to bubble. Cook until the mixture reaches between 120 and 130°C; the lower the temperature, the softer the toffee, so experiment a little. If there's any sugar on the insides on the pan, scrape it down to prevent crystallisation.

Take the toffee off the heat, leave for 5 minutes before adding the whisky (if you add it to a hot mixture the flavour will evaporate in a cloud of steam). Don't fret that the toffee is alcoholic; the alcohol will burn off and leave only the flavour.

Pour the toffee into the tray and, when it's cool enough, mark into squares. When Hazel makes the toffee she wraps each piece in a square of greaseproof paper, old-fashioned style.

TATTIES (LUCKY, TOBERMORY, MEALIE AND PEEDIE)

Scotland

Tatties, which come in various varieties, look rather like biscuits. They are a solid lump of grainy sugar and glucose, similar in texture to Edinburgh Rock and coated with a thick layer of ground cinnamon. It is not unlikely that tatties, like macaroons, once used potato as the main ingredient. Lucky tatties once contained toys (plastic soldiers and the like) or coins which are now outlawed under Health and Safety rules. Mealie Tatties contain oatmeal (and so could be considered the healthier alternative?), and the others are differentiated purely by packaging and place of origin; Peedie belongs to Orkney and Tobermory comes from that same island.

Tatties don't seem to exist much in captivity south of the Border, although they have been sighted, through binoculars, surreptitiously roaming the hills of Ireland, skulking behind bushes. They are quite, quite delicious, and if you want a colossal sugar hit, tatties are the bomb.

In the olden days, children pondering over how to extract the best value from their pennies in the sweetshop encountered something of a dilemma when contemplating the tattie. Because the tattie is large (about 7cm in diameter) compared to most sweets, it is relatively expensive; you could buy handfuls of smaller sweets for the whacking three pence demanded by purveyors of the ginormous tattie for a single sweet. The upside used to be that the lucky tattie, for example, contained a bonus treasure inside: a little plastic charm, much like the sort of thing that you get inside a Christmas cracker.

Monarch Confectionery in Troon is one of three Scottish sweet-makers still producing this sweet and the trays of beautiful fresh tatties that I saw there, with their generous coating of muddy-looking cinnamon, did actually resemble flattened baby new potatoes. Monarch also invented tiny tatties, a miniature alternative just 3cm across, which are easier to eat.

NB If the volume of cinnamon here seems excessive, don't worry. It's meant to be! Drifts of cinnamon floating in the air and settling on every surface of your kitchen is a likely by-product of making tatties.

Makes 25–30 burger-sized tatties

60ml golden syrup	250g icing sugar
60g soft butter	125g ground cinnamon

Pour the syrup into a large bowl and stir in the butter thoroughly. Sift in the icing sugar a little at a time until you have a stiff dough. Knead by hand, adding extra sugar until the mixture is no longer sticky.

Shape the dough into flattened discs of whatever size you like – traditional tatties are about the size of a burger. Then press them into a mound of cinnamon, covering all over. Tatties will keep indefinitely if stored, wrapped in greaseproof paper, in an airtight jar.

WALNUT WHIP
Edinburgh

Since its invention in 1910 by the now-defunct Duncan's of Edinburgh (a company actually founded in Dundee) the much-loved Walnut Whip has even made its way into the Cockney rhyming slang dictionary, used to describe a range of things: a sleep (as in 'kip'); an excess of hallucinogenic drugs ('trip',) and a vasectomy ('snip').

The walnut whip is a conical whirl of chocolate filled with a marshmallow-type fondant. The top of the whip is crowned with a half a walnut. Back in the day, the other half of the walnut waited, like hidden treasure, stuck on the inside base of the pyramid, awaiting the probing tongue of the delicate eater. Sadly, this walnut half was phased out sometime in the 1970s. Why? Health and safety? Production costs? Soaring costs of walnut halves? Maybe all of the above.

Walnut Whips are now made by Nestlé, who claim that one is eaten every two seconds in Britain. So I was absolutely astonished to find that my friends Saoirse and Colm, born at the turn of the millenium, had never actually tasted one until very recently.

In researching this sweet, I found another shocking fact. Did you know that an innocent walnut whip was used in an assassination attempt? It was a while ago now, but the information was highlighted in 2005 when it became available to the public.

In 1922, the Metropolitan Police Commissioner, Brigadier General Sir William Horwood, was pleased to receive an entire box of walnut whips. He assumed they were a present from his daughter Beryl, who, coincidentally, had told him that she'd sent something to him. However, after scoffing a few, the sweet-toothed police commissioner was writhing in agony. The confectionery looked normal but was later discovered to have been injected with deadly weedkiller. Furthermore, shortly afterwards, the real gift from Beryl arrived.

The devious mastermind behind the plot to kill Sir William was one Walter Tatam, about whom we sadly know very little. His plan didn't work, though. Neither did his attempts to murder other senior policemen by means of poisoned chocolate éclairs. Tatam's motive was unclear. He said that talking hedges told him to do it. The would-be assassin was later found to be quite, quite mad.

This will give you something to ponder on next time you bite off that walnut, nibble a hole in the top, and delve for the foamy filling with the tip of your tongue. Just avoid the talking hedges.

The prospect of making a walnut whip at home is just silly. Instead, try this delicious chocolate and walnut cake with a marshmallow filling, and the surprise of an actual walnut whip buried inside!

Walnut Whip Surprise Cake

Serves 8–10

50g cocoa powder, sifted
6 tbsp hot water
4 tbsp full-fat milk
175g self-raising flour
3 medium eggs
1 tsp baking powder
100g unsalted butter, at room
   temperature
300g golden caster sugar

150ml double cream
20g blanched whole walnuts
20g crushed walnuts
1 Walnut Whip
150g mini marshmallows
icing sugar, to dust
20 walnut halves, to decorate

two 20cm sandwich tins

Preheat the oven to 180°C/gas mark 4. Grease and line the tins.

In a large bowl, mix the cocoa powder and water, to make a paste. Add the milk, flour, eggs, baking powder, butter and caster sugar and beat well until all the ingredients are thoroughly mixed. Divide between the two tins and bake for 25–30 minutes until a skewer inserted into the centre comes out clean. Set aside on baking trays to cool completely in their tins.

Remove the cakes from their tins, cut a small hole in the centre of one of them, just the right size for the walnut on top of the walnut whip to peep through.

Whip the cream until it stands up in peaks, then stir in both types of walnuts.

Place the walnut whip in the centre of the cake without the hole and spread the cream mixture around it. Stud the cream with the marshmallows.

Carefully place the second cake on top so that the walnut peeks through, then decorate the edges with the walnut halves. Dust with icing sugar.

WINE GUMS
Stamford Hill, London

I distinctly remember my gran telling me that wine gums definitely contained wine, but that the practice was stopped because booze was too expensive to put into sweets. (Note she assumed the issue was about money rather than the rights or wrongs of feeding alcohol to kiddies.)

WINE GUMS
Stamford Hill, London

She was wrong, anyway. Wine gums have never contained wine or any other form of alcohol. But in some quarters the preconception remains. As recently as 2009 a 15-year-old boy hit the news on an international scale when, shopping for his wine gums in Wisbech, Cambridgeshire, he was prohibited from buying them by a careful shopkeeper, as the boy was clearly under age. Apparently, in Wisbech at that time, wine gums were right up there on the list of dangerous and subversive items prohibited to children, including hunting knives, guns, pornography and certain kinds of adhesives popular with glue-sniffing hobbyists.

Wine gums were the brainchild of Charles Gordon Maynard. Charles was the son of Charles Riley Maynard who, along with his brother, Tom, had started a small sweet-making enterprise in the kitchen of their house in Stamford Hill, London, in the 1880s. At this time the Temperance Movement had a firm hold in the UK and the Maynards followed the fashionable but possibly thumb-twiddling trend of being strictly teetotal Methodists. It's fair to say that the approach to alcohol among the Temperance set wasn't dissimilar to the general attitude that we have to crack cocaine today. So when Charles junior suggested the idea for the sweets to his straight-laced parents, his father was utterly outraged until his son hurriedly explained the reasoning behind such a seemingly controversial move (not forgetting the crucial fact that his proposed sweets didn't actually contain booze). Charles junior hoped that people might actually eschew booze in favour of his clever invention. The Maynards advertised wine gums as being so good, and so delicious, that they should be appreciated in exactly the same way as wine (except, presumably, without the hangover).

The appeal of the sweets, which would hopefully lure the hiccupping die-hard sots of late-Victorian Britain from their regular fix of adulterated spirits and various kinds of hooch, was enhanced by their different shapes and flavours, all of which bore raised lettering describing a type of alcohol. Is it likely that if wine gums had been invented more recently they might be prohibited under the Trade Descriptions Act?

By now, the question you're asking is, can I make wine gums at home?

Yes you can, but it's really not worth the bother. Rather, pick out 100g of your favourite flavour and pop them in a 750ml bottle of vodka for a day or two, after which they will have melted. A delicious, colourful tipple!

YELLOW MAN
Ballycastle, County Antrim

Lammas is the harvest festival celebrated in August and Yellow Man is a yellow, brittle honeycomb-like toffee that is traditionally served at the Lammas Fair in County Antrim. 'Did you treat your Mary Anne to Yellow Man, at the Lammas Fair, O?' It's the granddaddy of the commercial derivative that hides behind a cloak of chocolate as a Crunchie bar. The Crunchie may have inspired advertising jingles, but it never inspired an actual folksong as Yellow Man has, in 'The Ould Lammas Fair'.

Unlike other honeycombs, a distinctive feature of Yellow Man is the thick 'rind' that forms on its underside which often accounts for half the volume of the chunk. This happens when the toffee is knocked and the bubbles in the honeycomb burst. It is as unrelenting to bite into as a stick of rock.

If you want to have a go at making Yellow Man, you might well need to experiment, so you'll need tenacity. Then again, it might turn out perfectly the first time.

Before you start, here are some points to note:

It's essential that the mixture reaches 150°C (hard crack stage).

The bubbly texture of this sweet is an essential part of its character. What causes the bubbles? It's a reaction between the vinegar and the bicarbonate of soda, which distributes carbon dioxide gas throughout

YELLOW MAN
Ballycastle, County Antrim

the mixture. Vigorous stirring is essential. The more you stir, the more bubbles you'll make, and the lighter and lovelier the Yellow Man will be. A side effect is that a bubbly Yellow Man equals happy teeth.

The longer the bicarbonate of soda is cooked, the darker the mixture will be. You're aiming for a soft golden yellow, so be prepared to whisk hard and fast once you've added the bicarb.

After you've poured the Yellow Man into its cooling tray, you might be left with a denser mix at the bottom of the cooking pan. Pour this off separately into a different container.

40g Irish (or other) butter
250g demerara sugar
400g golden syrup
3 tbsp water

2 tbsp white wine or pale malt
   vinegar
1 tbsp bicarbonate of soda

20 x 20 x 5cm tray, buttered

Place the butter in a heavy-bottomed pan, attaching your sugar thermometer to the inside. Add the brown sugar, stir for a few moments, then dollop in the golden syrup. Heat gently over a medium heat until everything has dissolved.

Turn up the heat and allow the mixture to work itself up to the frenzy of a rolling boil. What you're looking for is zillions of tiny bubbles and a slight darkening of the mixture. Remember, this is Yellow Man, not brown man, and certainly not sunburned man. The sugar thermometer needs to read a clear 150°C (hard crack stage). As soon as this happens remove the pan from the heat immediately and carefully pour in the vinegar; the mixture will spit at you, so stand back and be very careful. Then add the bicarbonate of soda and stir with plenty of vim and vigour, making lots of froth as you do so.

Pour immediately into the buttered tray and leave to set. Be careful not to jog the tray. The toffee will sink a little as it cools, but if it collapses altogether then you added the bicarbonate of soda before the sugar mix was hot enough. This means you'll have to start all over again.

Yellow Man is at its best eaten on the day it's made. If you need to store it, put it into an airtight jar for up to five days. Any longer, and the toffee will go soft and squidgy.

BIBLIOGRAPHY AND THANKS

BIBLIOGRAPHY

The Accomplish't Cook, or, The Art and Mystery of Cookery... In Any Language, Robert May (originally published in 1660); Dodo Press, 2010

Come Hither – A Collection of Rhymes and Poems for the Young of All Ages, Walter de la Mare, Constable, 1923

The Complete Confectioner: Or the Whole Art of Confectionery Made Easy, Frederick Nutt (originally published in 1807) General Books, 2012

The Complete Confectioner, Pastry-Cook, and Baker, Eleanor Parkinson (originally published in 1844), Biblio Life, 2009

Favourite Sweets and Toffee Recipes, Carol Wilson, J. Salmon Ltd., 1998

First Catch Your Peacock, Bobby Freeman and Keith Morris, Y Lolfa, 2006

The Household Book of Lady Grisell Baillie, 1692-1733 Scottish Historical Society 1911

A Little History of Irish Food, Regina Sexton, Gill and Macmillan Ltd., 2001

London Labour and the London Poor (originally published in 1851), Henry Mayhew, Wordsworth Editions, 2008

The Scots Kitchen; Its Traditions and Lore with Old-Time Recipes, F. Marian NcNeill, Blackie and Son Ltd., 1929

Rural Rhymes and Sketches in East Lothian, Samuel Mucklebackit (originally published in 1885), Nabu Press, 2012

Skuse's Complete Confectioner, W.J. Bush and Company (Thirteenth Edition), 1957

The Sugar Barons, Matthew Parker, Windmill Books, 2011

Sugar-plums and Sherbet, Laura Mason, Prospect Books, 2004

Sweet Memories, Robert Opie, Anova Books, 1998

Sweetmeat-Making at Home, Mrs M. E. Rattray, Arthur Pearson Ltd., 1904

The Frugal Cook, E. Carter, 1851 Nabu Press, 2010

Sweets: A History of Temptation, Tim Richardson, Transworld, 2002

Sweet Talk, Nicholas Whittaker, Gollancz, 1998

Sylvia's Lovers, Elizabeth Gaskell (originally published in 1863), Oxford University Press, 1993

The Trebor Story, Matthew Crampton, Muddler Books, 2012

Online Resources

www.irishfoodguide.ie

www.wakefield.gov.uk

www.artsconnection.org.uk

www.stricklandgate-house.org.uk

www.bedfordmuseum.org

www.rampantscotland.com

www.visityork.org

www.kendalmintcake.net

www.alangeorge.co.uk

www.angus.gov.uk

www.bbc.co.uk

As well as the URLs listed here, I accessed numerous online discussions and found a wealth of information as well as help from many of their members. Thanks to all of you.

THANK YOU

To Liam. Also to Peter Casaru, David Meacham, Karin Mear, Nigel Evans, Fiona Bird, Audrey Gillan, Jeanne McKenzie, Carol Wilson, Connie Duffy and Zack Gallagher, Jeremy Dee of Swizzels Matlow and Rachael Richards at RMS PR. I'd also like to thank the splendid team at the Abergavenny Food Festival who gave SweetieFest the best launch ever!

Susie and James Suter and Karl Cheetham at Gliffaes Country House Hotel (who so very kindly and foolhardily lent me their kitchen for recipe testing). Cath and Steve Maggs ... Maybe next time? Amanda at The Pot and Pineapple in Abergavenny and Mel at Candyland in Brecon. Jules, Kathy and Brett at Black Mountain Gold in Crickhowell. All the lovely girls at Brecon Beacons Holiday Cottages. Deby, John and Mia. H.G. Ritchie of Dublin. Martin Stimson at Impex Management. Tanya Braun at Richmond Towers Communication and all at Fisherman Friend in Lofthouse. Mariana Wall at Luther Pendragon and Cristiana Schwab at Wrigley's. Dave Healy, Ted and Betty at Grays of Dudley. All at Aunty Sandra's Candy Factory, Belfast, especially David and Jim Moore.

Isabel Atherton and James Duffett-Smith. Rosemary Davidson, Imogen Fortes, Alun Owen, Clara Womersley, Ruth Waldram, Lisa Gooding and all at Square Peg/Penguin Random House. Alexandra, Frank and Tom at www.alexandramarr.com – truly stellar people.

Kendal to Hull road trip

John, Paula, Max and Evan Barron and all at Romney's, especially Malcolm. Farrah's of Harrogate, the York Tourist Board, Robert Copley and all at Farmer Copleys. Tim and Anne- Marie Jibson, Burnsy, Helen Scholefield, Joan Venus-Evans and all at Radio Humberside; Mike

Covell, Nicky Holthuysen, Sue Rogers, June Reeve, Mike Bickerstaff, Pauline Steenson, Jean Reeve, Olive Walker, Kitty Shackleton, Jean Spicer, Angela Martin, Jessie Thompson. Also huge thank to my Dad, Trevor Nozedar, Maureen, Mark, Kerry and Megan.

Wales road trip

Hazel Thomas and Anwyn at the National Library of Wales. Alison Kidd, Peter Williams and all at Talybont-On-Usk Energy. Stephen Bray and all at Brays of Newport (www.thewelshsweetshop.com). Fred Bray, Jason Bray, Laura Bray, Thomas Bray and Benedict Bray. The Conservative Club, Merthyr Tydfil. Julie Bell, Makthie and all at the Felinfach Griffin (www.eatdrinksleep.com). Steve and Freya at Ella Rileys (www.ellarileysweets.com). Martin Orbach at Shepherds Ices, Hay-on-Wye.

Scotland road trip

Chris Husband, Gordon and all at Candyco/Monarch Confectionery. Sandra Fisher, Mary Davidson, Andrena Bain, Crawford Rae and Douglas Rae and all at Buchanans and Golden Casket. Sunny Pahuja, Jeanette and all at Nisha Enterprises. Alison Clark. Alistair Morgan. Claire Ross and Scott Renton, Elspeth and Ronnie. Agnes and Niall MacFarlane. Derek Shaw and Gloria Shaw.

Finally, to all the sweet makers of Britain, past and present ... Thank you!

YOUR RECIPE NOTES

YOUR RECIPE NOTES